THE RAIDERS
OF ARAKAN

T. B.

T. B

C. E. LUCAS PHILLIPS

THE RAIDERS

OF ARAKAN

With a Foreword by
Admiral of the Fleet
The Earl Mountbatten of Burma, K.G.

HEINEMANN : LONDON

William Heinemann Ltd
15 Queen Street, Mayfair, London W1X 8BE

LONDON MELBOURNE TORONTO

JOHANNESBURG AUCKLAND

First published 1971

© C. E. Lucas Phillips 1971

434 43657 7

Printed in Great Britain by
Cox & Wyman Ltd, London, Fakenham
and Reading

Foreword

by

Admiral of the Fleet The Earl Mountbatten of Burma, K.G.

The Commanding Officer of a battalion whom I addressed in Burma in 1943, shortly after setting up the Supreme Allied Command in South-East Asia, told me many years later of the impact my remarks had had. He reminded me that I started my talk: 'I hear you call this the Forgotten Front. I hear you call yourselves the Forgotten Army. Well, let me tell you that this is not the Forgotten Front, and you are not the Forgotten Army. In fact, nobody has even heard of you.'

He says this caused quite a stir and a shock until I went on: 'But they will hear of you very soon when you start beating the Japs and they will never forget you.'

This I am sure is true of the Fourteenth Army as a whole and the allied sailors and airmen who fought alongside them, but I am afraid it is not wholly true of some of the bravest and most effective small units who fought under my command; notably V Force, who collected invaluable intelligence at great risk on the Arakan Front.

It is time the story of their heroism was told, so that they may never be forgotten and Brigadier Lucas Phillips has told it uncommonly well in *The Raiders of Arakan*.

Of the many thousands I met in Burma few made a deeper impression on me than Denis Holmes. This story is largely about his exploits.

I am delighted that included in this account of V Force are details of their operations with the 3rd Commando Brigade and Units of the 81st West African Division, for these are splendid examples of the enthusiastic co-operation which existed between such diverse forces in the South-East Asia Command.

I welcome this exciting book.

Mountbatten of Burma

A.F.

Contents

Preamble

This narrative records the exploits of a very little-known, para-military unit and of the British and West African soldiers whom they served on the Arakan coast of Burma.

The unit, one of several of what was known as V Force, was composed chiefly of peasants, fishermen and the like and was commanded by Major (now Lt-Colonel) Denis Holmes. Their business, in default of a properly organized Intelligence service, was to gather information of the enemy's activities in and immediately behind his fighting front and to convey it to the British side. Their daring was remarkable, their information usually of exemplary accuracy and their speed instant. Their story and the stories of the soldiers whom they often accompanied into battle have remained in undeserved obscurity, which this narrative is designed to penetrate.

For all major incidents and particularly for the operations of the Commandos there is excellent documentation, the Commandos' records being available in great detail. For the activities of his unit of V Force there is Major Holmes's reliable diary, supplemented by the narrative account that he wrote immediately afterwards. In many matters of detail, however, reliance has had to be placed on personal memories, which are not always infallible, though they have been sifted and tested as searchingly as is possible.

To this extent, therefore, the narrative here presented is not to be regarded as an exact military history, but as an endeavour to present a true general account of remarkable minor operations by men of strangely mixed origins, colours and creeds; but all, be it remembered, inspired by faith in British leadership and example.

The chief sources of information are set out in page 191. The reader not familiar with military matters, particularly the Indian Army of those days, is referred to the Appendices.

C. E. LUCAS PHILLIPS

I

What Happened in Burma

The Dark Hour – The Scene of the Conflict
The Offensive that Failed

The rain crashed down in a barrage of massive violence. It beat
down upon all hard surfaces like the clamour of a hundred guns
and upon all vegetation like rapid fire from a thousand rifles.
Within minutes it turned the long-parched earth into a morass
and within an hour the dry watercourses into swirling torrents.
The monsoon of 1943 had begun in Arakan.

At the door of his bamboo hut Major Denis Holmes, wet to
the skin, surveyed the scene with gloomy feelings. A Regular
Service officer in the 1st Punjab Regiment, thirty years old, of
wiry figure, below middle height, he had spent three and a half
years of the war without having fired a shot. Until a few days
before he had been tediously employed in the command of a
light anti-aircraft battery in an inactive role 600 miles away in
Central India, a role to which the 8th battalion of his regiment
had been converted.

The war, he felt, was passing him by. Having been seconded
to the Assam Rifles, which was an armed gendarmerie, he had
also, to his chagrin, missed service with his own battalion in
Abyssinia and in the Western Desert, where they had added
fresh lustre to the pages of their history.

With ten years regular service behind him, he felt himself
completely out of it. He was eager to become an infantryman
again and to engage the Japanese at close quarters. Thus he had
obeyed with alacrity the order posting him to the 2nd battalion
of his regiment, then fighting in Arakan, only to find himself
caught up in the tail of yet another melancholy failure of

British arms. Instead of joining 2nd/1st Punjabis, hard pressed in the battlefront, he was diverted to act as a liaison officer for an emergency force under a commander for whom he felt little affection.

The Dark Hour

The fortunes of Britain and her Allies in this sector of the world's battlefields lay still in darkness. The sad tale had begun fourteen months earlier, when, as part of the greatest act of aggression in the world's history, the Japanese had made their surprise invasions, without cause, on ten territories simultaneously, of which Burma was one. Merciless, brutal, hardy, brave, 'savages equipped with modern arms', inspired by the Japanese equivalent of Nazism, they had made rings round the scratch force of half-trained British, Indian, Burmese and American-led Chinese troops, wholly unequipped for jungle warfare, under an extemporized General Headquarters totally inappropriate to war and entirely lacking an Intelligence Service.

There had followed the longest and most heartbreaking retreat in British history, from the extreme south to the extreme north of Burma, extending to more than 1,000 miles in four months, skilfully conducted under the command of General Alexander, with Lt-General Bill Slim as Corps Commander.[1] Nearly all the Burmese deserted and slunk off to their homes; nearly all the Chinese turned tail and fled at breakneck speed at the mere approach of the enemy. The British and Indians fought back, usually in good order, some of them superbly, protecting and succouring as best they could hundreds of thousands of distressed refugees – Indians, Burmese and British – flying from the wrath of the Japanese. At the end of the Great Retreat those of the British-Indian troops who remained marched over the northern mountain barrier into India in rags and sodden by the monsoon rains, but soldiers still, in good order, carrying their arms and obedient to their officers.

Of the various causes of this failure, one of the most significant had been the total absence of any Intelligence Service to keep

[1] Other armies have of course, incurred far longer retreats, notably the German retreats from Alamein and from Stalingrad.

Alexander informed of the enemy's movements. There had followed, during the ensuing monsoon months of 1942 (when all major hostilities were suspended by both sides), deep heart-searching by the British and Americans in London, Washington and Delhi and throughout the whole of the forces in India, where the impressive figure of General Sir Archibald Wavell, revered, austere, sphinx-like, was Commander-in-Chief. Denied the material and human resources that he needed by the Chiefs of Staff in Washington and London for what they rated as a minor campaign, Wavell passionately sought a bold and decisive offensive, but was driven to accept minor ones only.

Dominant in his mind was the need for a quick victory, in order to restore the morale of the Indian forces, badly shaken by the harsh reverses of the Great Retreat, particularly (as nearly always occurs) among those troops that had not yet done any fighting. A large part of the Indian Army, shaken by stories of the Great Retreat, true and false, had been gripped by an unreasoning fear of the Japanese and by an equal fear of the terrors of the jungle. The knowledge that the Japanese murdered the wounded and treated prisoners with brutal severity did nothing to encourage a fighting spirit.

This malaise Wavell and his subordinate generals determined to stamp out. Men must be inspired with confidence that they could beat the Japanese. They must learn to make the jungle their friend, not to regard it as an enemy. New divisions were formed and all went into intensive training in jungle fighting, learning to live hard and to move quickly with the minimum of gear. Mules replaced most of the regimental motor transport. Something must be attempted to build up some sort of Intelligence Service.

As the rain poured down Wavell spread out his few divisions and his meagre air squadrons thinly along the 600 miles of the India-Burma boundary, which stretched from Arakan on the Bay of Bengal, up over the great mountain barrier and so to the borders of China, where the anglophobe American General Stilwell commanded the rabble that composed the army of Chiang Kai-shek. In the centre, based on the romantic mountain state of Manipur, but ravaged by sickness in the malarial and rain-sodden valleys ahead where they bickered with the enemy, stood Geoffrey Scoones's 4th Corps, destined before long to fight one of the great battles of history in and around Kohima and Imphal.

To the Arakan front, 300 miles from Manipur, Wavell sent, as commander of 15th Corps, the most significant of all personalities in the long story of the Burma war, Lt-General Bill Slim, the bulldog figure that inspired so much confidence wherever it was seen and whose steadiness, resourcefulness and quick thinking had already been made manifest in the crises of the Retreat. It was on this front, with the object of gaining a quick victory, that Wavell had decided to make one of the two limited offensives to which he had been reduced and it is with a corner of the craggy terrain that we shall henceforth be concerned in this narrative.

The Scene of the Conflict

Arakan is a province of Burma that has a character all its own. Spiny, horny, coarse-grained, it lies astride that great spur of the Himalayas which divides India from Burma where it turns south to thrust its bristly feet into the waters of the Bay of Bengal. The Southern limb of this range, known as the Arakan Yomas, marches some miles inland, but westward it spreads out gnarled fingers that clasp a complex of rivers where they pour into the bay. Notice especially the long finger called the Mayu (or 'Mad Woman') Range, which lies between the parallel rivers Mayu and Naf, for it is here that our battles are to be fought. A third river, the Kaladan, which lies east of the Mayu, has a more distant relevance to our narrative. *See Fig. 2.*

All the features – the rivers and the forked branches of the mountains – run north and south, so that, as the monsoon sweeps in from the bay from late April till October it surges against the razor-ridged hills and precipitates itself in one of the highest incidences of rainfall in the world. In six months 200 inches of rain descend. In April it comes in occasional short, violent downpours of a few hours or days, known as the 'mango showers', for it is then that the fruits of the big mango trees drop. In May the rain becomes almost continuous, beating down with terrific violence. In one day (5 November), as

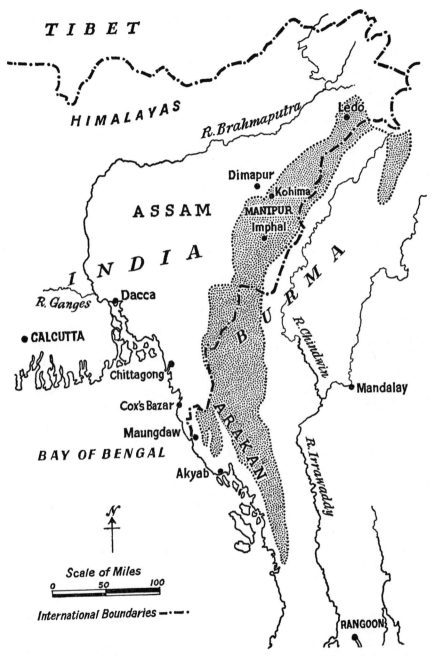

Fig. 1. The theatre of operations in the Burma campaigns of 1941–45,
showing the great mountain barrier along the frontier between Burma
and India.

General Lloyd's division was moving painfully southwards for the Arakan offensive, the rainfall measured 13 inches.

All the hills are densely clothed with jungle, dark as night, right up to their sharp, spiny ridges. Large stretches are covered with thickets of bamboo and monster elephant grass, through which progress is impossible until a way is hacked out by axe, machete or the long, broad-bladed *dah* that all Burmese carry. Elsewhere the trees vary greatly and everywhere giant creepers entangle the feet or hang down from the branches as thick as curtains. No one lives in the dark, steep mountain jungles of the Mayu peninsula. Thus, what with the craggy ground and the thick jungle, movement is difficult everywhere, with no means of progress other than rough footpaths and bullock-cart tracks, except for one short road that we shall notice later.

However, unlike most records of the arduous war in Burma, in these pages we shall not often be plunged into the dark entanglements of the jungle, but shall be more intimately concerned with that narrow strip of coastal plain which flanks the eastern bank of the River Naf, where its muddy waters, slithering with jellyfish at certain seasons, roamed by the mahseer and the occasional shark, and gleaming at night with flashes of phosphorescent light, race out into the great expanse of the Bay of Bengal. Here the spiky, jungle-clad hills of the Mayu Range level out to form a fertile, sandy terrain only two or three miles wide. It is here that people live, tilling the soft soil or reaping the harvest of the sea. They live in somewhat densely packed villages and the majority of their houses are built of bamboo, thatched with palm-leaves, and stand on stilts as a protection against the floods that rise and surge under the monsoon rains.

These houses are known as *bashas*, a term that will constantly occur in these pages. They stood among plantations of divers and profitable trees, notably the sumptuous mango and the big banyan, beneath the ample foliage of which the villager and his small hump-back cattle found relief from the heat of the sun in the dry season.

Palms abound, particularly the small betel-palm, the nuts of which constitute the chewing-gum of these regions, staining the lips and teeth a brilliant scarlet. Banana trees flourish among all the dwellings, their big, flopping, pale-green leaves looking fresh and cool as a wind fans them. The kanyin, or wood-oil tree is a characteristic of parts of the battlefield to come, and so is the ginger bush. Bamboo is everywhere, in dense, rattling thickets or lonely clumps, its strong, erect wood put to many uses. The bashas of Muslim families stand within compounds that are enclosed by high bamboo fences, strictly guarding their women from public view.

All around the village lie the paddy-fields, in which rice of fine quality is grown. The paddy is dead flat, but each field is surrounded by a *bund*, or bank, two to three feet high, built to retain the water when the fields are flooded by the monsoon rains. The farmer ploughs with oxen in April and plants out his rice seedlings when the paddy is flooded.

The tidy pattern of the rice-fields on the coastal plain, however, is deeply cleft on the eastern side of the Naf by innumerable watercourses that are tributary to it. The term for a watercourse of this sort is a *chaung*, corresponding to the Indian *nullah* and the *wadi* of Arabic lands. Unlike the chaungs inland, they never run dry near the coast in the rainless months, but are tidal and so are filled with water when the sea is at the flood and still hold some water or become beds of deep, oozy mud when the sea ebbs. On the coastal plain they twist and curl back on themselves in a serpentine and most confusing manner and, although sometimes fordable to men on foot, are a serious obstacle to the progress of armies, having virtually no bridges. Thus troops carrying out offensive operations had frequently to be supplied with native sampans, a requirement that became one of the manifold tasks of Denis Holmes. In many places near the coast these chaungs pass through very low-lying areas which are large expanses of mud but become one with the sea when the tide flows. Indeed, in the country that we shall have to travel mud is second only to the wind-blown sand.

Until it reaches the open sea, the Naf is bordered in many places by dense groves of mangrove swamp. They are bottomed by black, stinking mud, from which the sombre and ungainly mangrove trees rise in serried phalanxes. To the ordinary eye they have a nasty and sinister air, but to Holmes and his native scouts their dark obscurity served to provide secret ports of entry behind the enemy lines and refuges in which they could lie up unseen.

The rains, the river and the vegetation govern the climate and the way of life. From November till February the weather is agreeably cool, but in late March it becomes oppressively hot, dry and dusty, with pre-monsoon winds that are like the breath of a furnace. Once the monsoon starts the heat is aggravated by the dense humidity. Clothing and blankets and all fabric are permanently damp. Boots, belts and saddlery become green with mould. The smell of dampness is in everyone's nostrils. In the pauses of the rain, the moisture from the hot, wet earth evaporates in white, woolly clouds, like a ground mist.

Even in the dry season, desiccated though the land is for most of the time, watery phenomena persist disagreeably in the morning until dispelled by the fierce heat of the sun. The night dews are astonishingly heavy, crashing down among the foliage in such volume as to smother conversation, and dense, cold, breast-high mists collect at night and last a few hours after dawn until well into March.

This heat and the humidity occasion various distressing diseases, particularly malaria and dysentery, foster noxious creatures of diverse sorts, such as the anopheles mosquitoes, leeches, typhus-bearing ticks and the occasional snake, but these are more prevalent in the hill-jungle astride and east of the Mayu Range than on the western coastal plain.

With this outline picture in mind, it is no surprise that Arakan is a primitive, inhospitable, sparsely populated province and that its people are a peculiar mixture of shrewd intelligence and primitive habits among whom animal passions run high. The two main strains of the population, mutually hostile, divided by race, language and religion, were of Muslim and Buddhist persuasions respectively.

The Buddhists, to whom the term 'Arakanese' was in these parts specially applied, belonged to a tribe or strain known as Maughs or Mughs. In general, they were indolent, pleasure-loving, treacherous and pro-Japanese. Most of them had smooth, hairless faces. They, and especially their women, were keen chewers of the betel-nut, which stained their lips a vivid red and charged their spittle, which they expectorated frequently, with the colour of an advanced tuberculosis. They loved bright colours and ornaments, as manifested in the men's calf-length *lungyis* and in the women's red drapes, ear-rings, bangles and the flowers in their black, glossy, high-piled hair, their *panache* accentuated by their love of cigars.

The Muslims had their origin in the District of Chittagong, in the Bengal Province of British India, and all Muslims, whether natives of Arakan for generations or recent immigrants, were known as Chittagonians, or in the British forces, as 'CFs'. They were poor, thrifty, hard-working, peaceful, superstitious, stoical in adversity and nearly all were completely loyal to the British, who protected them from Mugh oppression, and they frequently risked life, liberty and all that they possessed in the Allied cause. They were to become the most trusted and fearless of Denis Holmes's scouts. Masters of intrigue and deception, the Chittagonians made extremely good Intelligence agents behind the enemy lines but, when it came to a clash of interests among themselves, they quarrelled violently and were awful liars.

A bewildering babel of languages was spoken by these people. The Arakanese spoke a dialect of Burmese, but the Chittagonians stuck to the Bengali of their former homeland, but, if educated, spoke Urdu as well. The official language of British Burma was pure Burmese, so that a man might speak three or even four languages. Confusingly, place names often had more than one form; but in these pages they will have the style and spelling used in the British Cabinet Office official histories.

To readers of English many of these names have the most forbidding appearances but the British soldier, studying the seemingly crazy maps, with their dense maze of contour lines, their serpentine chaungs and their crackjaw names, found his own ways of overcoming this difficulty and we shall very often follow his example in order to make the flow of our narrative the smoother. Thus, to quote the most celebrated instance, Ngakyedauk, which gave its name to one of the most spectacular of battles, appropriately became 'Okydoke'. In like manner, the little, mud-girt island of Nahkaungdo, which in a special sense was Denis Holmes's discovery, obviously became 'No-Can-Do'.

Others readily adapt themselves to straight translations, such as 'Pumpkin Hill' and 'The Village of the Light of God'.

With the departure of the Anglo-Burmese civil administration in the face of Japanese invasion, chaos and bloodshed had spread throughout the quarrelsome province, beginning with the slaughter of the hapless Indian refugees fleeing from the Japanese terror in Burma and afterwards taking the shape of a bloodthirsty civil war between the Maughs and the Muslims; when the latter had been worsted in the south the Maughs proceeded to fight among themselves.

Yet in normal times the pursuits of these fierce and somewhat treacherous people were peaceful enough. In all the river valleys and wherever a piece of flat ground offered itself they cultivated rice in the banked paddy-fields. Generally, the Arakanese owned the land and the Chittagonians tilled it for them. The Chittagonians engaged also in fishing and were expert watermen, particularly in the use of the primitive dug-out canoe that they called a *kisti*, of which Holmes and his friends were to make frequent use in their prowls along the enemy flanks.

The Offensive that Failed

The Arakan offensive that Wavell had ordered to be launched – known as First Arakan – was entrusted to 14th Indian Division (Major-General Wilfred Lloyd), under the direct orders of Eastern Army, cutting out Slim and his 15th Corps. Air support was provided by Air Commodore Gray's 224 Group, RAF. The intention was to overrun the ninety miles of the Mayu Peninsula, not strongly held by the enemy, and to capture the island of Akyab at the tip of the peninsula.

Having moved southwards laboriously from India across roadless country, but helped by an improvised, soldier-manned 'navy' of assorted small craft, 14th Division began their offensive in December. Moving along either side of the knife-edge of the Mayu Range and astride the Mayu River, they clambered over the steep and wooded slopes and across the watery chaungs, provisioned laboriously by mules, porters and native sampans. The central spine of the range, however, was left untenanted,

Fig. 2. Zone of operations of 15th Corps.

being judged too precipitous and too matted with jungle, so that the columns working down on east and west were not in close contact.

At first all went well. By 1 January 1943 very nearly the whole of the Mayu Peninsula had been overrun, but from that moment everything went wrong. Unseasonable rains washed away the makeshift roads and bridges behind the forward troops and in the resulting delay the Japanese pushed in reinforcements by sea from their Akyab garrison, and rapidly built up a formidable complex of bunkers at Donbaik on the west and at Rathedaung ('Hermit's Hill') on the east. It was the first time that the remarkable Japanese bunkers had been encountered. British and Indian troops of good quality and much superior in numbers attacked again and again with great gallantry and heavy losses against a seemingly invulnerable enemy.

Worse was to follow. Determined to hold Arakan as one of his chief defensive bastions, the commander of the Japanese 1st Army, General Iida, ordered forward 55th Division, under Lt-General Takishi Koga, from Central Burma, together with 5th Air Division to terrorize the civilians of Calcutta and Chittagong. Koga's troops first struck in the rear of the Indian brigade on the east of the Mayu range, disrupting them. Then, in one of the most audacious exploits of the war, a column led by the remarkable Colonel Tanahashi scaled the precipitous and untenanted mountain spine, descended on the west side and in the early hours of 5 April, surprised the headquarters of the British 6th Brigade under Brigadier Cavendish, capturing the brigadier and then killing him.

Both brigades were cut off in the southern part of the peninsula. The Indian Brigade, severely mauled in difficult country, ceased to exist, but 6th Brigade, which Koga had intended to destroy, remained steady, collected itself in good order under Colonel B. H. Hopkins and fought its way out under the covering fire of the guns of 130th Field Regiment.

For a while 14th Division stabilized on a new line which the Army Commander ordered should be held in the approaching monsoon months. In this process it was relieved by General Lomax's 26th Division, wearing its badge of a Bengal tiger. All seemed secure, but an attempt to lure the Japanese into a large-scale ambush failed and enabled them to breach the new line in considerable length.

Slim, who had been keeping closely in touch with events, but strangely forbidden to influence them, was at long last allowed to take operational control early in May. With bitterness of heart, he found that he now had no option but to order a withdrawal right back to the open country of Cox's Bazar in India, with light forces forward at Bawli Bazar, just inside the Arakan frontier. Not only had the monsoon begun, but also he saw that, with some honourable exceptions, nearly all the troops were badly shaken and in no shape to undertake further serious fighting.

The situation was galling. It was 1942 all over again. We were back whence we had started after yet another retreat. Significantly, one of the prime causes of the failure, as in the Retreat, had been the complete lack of an organized Intelligence Service to give timely notice of enemy movements and intentions.

From the far eastern flank of the Allied forces there was also ill news. The offensive that Stilwell's Chinese were expected to undertake never even started. But there was something on the credit side. The first Chindit operation, under that strangely obsessed personality, Orde Wingate, although it had achieved nothing tactically, had at least proved that ordinary troops, when hard trained and well led by officers with plenty of guts, could penetrate deep into the enemy country and defeat those troops whom they met.

Further on the credit side, though Holmes and his brother officers did not yet know it, was that the Arakan operation, by drawing off the Japanese 55th Division, had forced the enemy to abandon their own planned offensive against the main central front in Manipur, which, if it had been successful, would have been damaging in the extreme to Wavell's hopes for the future.

2

Introduction to Battle

It was shortly before the withdrawal of 26th Indian Division to Cox's Bazar that Denis Holmes made his appearance upon the Arakan scene. Son of a retired Burma civil servant, he was a typical product of the Indian Army in its golden days. Professionally well trained, keen on games, fit and hardy, remarkably energetic, swift to act, sometimes hasty, he was of good breeding, quick at languages and a practising Christian in the Roman faith. Fond of good company, good food and drink, he could on occasions fall into a reserve, so that Antony Brett-James was later to describe him as 'the quiet major'. He was a bachelor and so far had no stronger feelings towards womankind than an occasional *tendresse* for one or other of the fair creatures adorning the British military and administration circles. Inevitably he was often called 'Sherlock' by his friends, though even more often it was 'Watson', which later became his code name.

Obedient to the order posting him to 2nd/1st Punjabis, Holmes left the staleness of Central India with relief, accompanied by his remarkable orderly, Khyber Khan, who was carrying his officer's bedding roll. Khyber was a tall Hazarawal Pathan from the North-West Frontier. A good Muslim and a fine rifle shot, he was very intelligent and utterly trustworthy. His devotion to Holmes had no limit. He was to serve him not only in Arakan, but also afterwards in the Italian campaign, back in India again after the war and finally, at the end of Holmes's service, as a civilian in Kuwait.

Holmes was therefore very distressed when, in changing trains at night in the long journey to the front, he lost contact with Khyber and so also with his bedding. His bedding he could replace, but not Khyber Khan. He had too much faith in him to imagine that Khyber would have absconded and his faith was justified many months later in a remarkable manner.

The 600-mile journey took a fortnight of dreary travel: ten days of stifling heat and dust in the slothful Indian railways as far as Chittagong, a day by sea from there to Cox's Bazar and thenceforward by a vile, makeshift road over which he bumped and jolted in a lorry, in clouds of dust. All the way, particularly from Chittagong onwards, Holmes was disturbed by the mood of depression and apathy that hung in the air. In Chittagong itself the civilians were in a state of jitters after a trivial bombing raid and wherever soldiers were congregated together he found no animation and no humour. The hot, miserable transit camps were breeding-grounds of inertia, the tents ragged, the huts dilapidated, with earth floors, all given over to the mosquito and flies, to the pervading dust and to the stale smell of lethargy.

What was wrong? Even a subaltern of his own regiment whom he met was affected. 'We're all worn out,' he said and found it hard to believe that Holmes was mad keen to get to the front. Equally surprised had been the camp commandant at Chittagong when Holmes inquired about means of getting forward and said: 'I want to get up the line as soon as possible.'

'Nobody wants to get up there, my dear fellow,' replied the commandant. 'They all want to come back. But don't let me deter you.'

Only occasionally did Holmes meet evidence of good morale and these were not of the sort to be first expected. One was the tall and cheerful Pathan captain who commanded the lorry convoy from Cox's Bazar onwards and the other, perhaps surprisingly, was the Indian Pioneer battalion, commanded, he was told, by a 'dug-out' colonel of the Guards, who was determined to get himself as far forward as his years allowed and who was not only doing the best he could to maintain the makeshift roads with the worst tools in the world, but also upheld a high standard of smartness and discipline under great difficulties. Holmes reflected caustically that the Colonel Blimps of Britain were doing a damned sight more for their country than many of those who poked fun at them.

At last the lorry convoy lurched into Burma and Holmes beheld with surprise what was the crowning example of improvisation by an army deprived of modern tools. Approaching the threshold of what was to become his own stamping ground, he saw a big chaung known as the Pruma, which, though some one hundred yards wide and, though vital to the army as carrying its only road, was spanned merely by a rickety bridge built of bamboo. It squeaked and groaned as Holmes's vehicle crawled over. In after years he smiled reminiscently at the much more substantial 'Bridge over the River Kwai'.

Beyond the rickety bridge he came to a large agglomeration of the stilted bamboo houses that he was to know as bashas, with a Buddhist pagoda and monastery and a tin-roofed school, all sizzling in the oppressive pre-monsoon heat. This was Bawli Bazar ('The Market-place of the Wrestlers'), which he was later to know as the headquarters of the special force in which he was to serve. Here the convoy swung south on the hot and dusty track to Maungdaw. As he passed the dry, baked paddy-fields and the numerous oozy chaungs, where parrots, green pigeons and gorgeous butterflies flapped and darted, Holmes looked with interest at the steep, saw-edged hills of the Mayu Range to his left. In his service with the Assam Rifles he had been familiar with the magnificent hill-jungle of Assam, often several thousand feet high, clothed in many places with splendid magnolias and rhododendrons, but this Mayu jungle was different. It looked harsh, forbidding, almost black and just as oppressively hot as down on the blown, sandy soil of the coastal plain.

Thus, after two days of this sweating, rattle-bone journey, Holmes came at last, among swirling clouds of dust, to one of the critical centres of the Arakan campaign and one that he was to know particularly well: Maungdaw. It is so important to our narrative that we must have a close look at it at once.

Maungdaw, as Holmes saw it, was a sprawling, dusty town situated at the point where the Tat Chaung (a name of importance) flows into the Naf, its crowded bamboo bashas interspersed here and there with timber-built storehouses and public buildings. Large expanses of malodorous grey mud stretched to north and south of it at low tide, but a jigsaw of chaungs made it appear to be an island when the tide rose high and at such times, being embowered in splendid mangoes, golden mohrs and pink and yellow cassias and set against the background of the 'Mad Woman' hills, it looked to the eye of the approaching traveller to be a picture-postcard place, an impression that was quickly dispelled on encountering its sharp odours, its flies, its clogging dust and its close, quivering heat.

In the total absence of good roads, the military value of Maungdaw was as a port. Makeshift though it was, with only a small, wooden jetty and ramshackle wharves, usable only by small craft, it nevertheless enabled stores and reinforcements to be brought close to the field of operations from the ports of India, thus avoiding the frequent transhipments of the train-sea-road journey that Holmes had undergone. It was served by the scratch flotilla of assorted small craft that we have already noticed.

Maungdaw thus became a large military emporium. Furthermore, it was the western terminal of the only road that traversed the Mayu Hills. This road was a disused railway track that twisted and turned through the tortuous spurs of the hills and burrowed under them in tunnels at two places, before reaching its eastern terminal, which was the large Buddhist village of Buthidaung ('Pumpkin Hill'), lying on that stretch of river where the Mayu changes its name to the Kalapanzin, which stands for 'Black Waters'.

This road from Maungdaw to Buthidaung was commonly called 'the tunnels road'. Obviously it was important to any army as providing the only good means of lateral communication, but, furthermore, it traversed a terrain that was of great tactical value: a terrain of fierce, jagged, steep mountain peaks draped with dark and sombre jungle to their very summits. Astride this range, with its well-protected lateral road, any army could build a formidable defensive system. This was the line that the Army Commander had ordered to be held for the monsoon period after the Japanese break-in in early April and it was the line that both armies were to strive to possess in the forthcoming battles.

Holmes found Maungdaw to be a dust-bowl, with quantities of troops at the transit camp who seemed to have lost their units. He was assailed with misgivings at their low morale and spent a restless night in a dug-in tent. Twice there was a stand-to, with the jittery rifle fire at nothing that is characteristic of ill-trained troops. He very much missed his faithful Khyber Khan and wondered what had become of him.

With relief, he made his way from this place of nerves early next morning to divisional headquarters, which was not far off and where an air of calm prevailed. He found that 14th Division was in process of handing over to 26th and was told by Colonel Cotterill-Hill, the able, crisply-spoken staff officer whom Slim had lent to General Lomax, that it was now impossible for him to get through to 2nd/1st Punjab.

Holmes's heart sank. Was he again to be denied? But Cotterill-Hill went on:

'However, I've another job going if you'd care for it.'

Holmes waited for him to explain.

'There's an *ad hoc* outfit the other side of the hills called Mayforce. Under Brigadier Curtis. He is in command of all the ops on that side of the Mayu Range. Virtually a division. He has asked for an experienced chap to act as liaison officer between him and his forward brigades and units. D'you fancy that?'

Eager to get forward, Holmes readily agreed. As soon as he could he made his way, by the Tunnels road, to the headquarters of Mayforce, which was in some paddy-fields near the village of Letwedet, a little west of 'Pumpkin Hill'. It was his first experience of active service and he was relieved to find a small, orderly, well-run camp, well camouflaged, of tents and bashas. There was no flap here. After the dark jungle and the steep drop from the tunnels road, the scene was agreeably open and sloped away gently to the east and to the picturesque township of Buthidaung, its pumpkins not apparent, but embowered in green foliage and its pagoda dominating its crowded bamboo houses on the banks of the Kalapanzin. For the first time, he heard the sound of guns in action away to the south.

It was damnably hot and close – the worst time of the year –

and the air was clouded with mosquitoes. The troops were wearing khaki drill shirts and shorts or trousers, but at night arms and legs must be fully covered and faces and hands painted with the sweet-smelling mosquito repellant. Men slept under short, khaki-coloured mosquito-nets, which they fixed as best they could, and night sentries were provided with veils. In spite of these precautions and of the daily tablet of mepacrin, the casualties from malaria were very heavy. So they were from dysentery. Sickness casualties were higher than battle casualties.

He met Curtis, who told him crisply what was expected of him: he was to keep personal touch with forward brigades and units, taking them his orders and bringing back information of their dispositions, their strengths, their requirements in ammunition and stores, and reporting on their morale.

'You must be ready to go anywhere any time of day or night,' Curtis told him, 'and make your own way forward as quickly as you can. You will speak with my authority. I must know exactly what is going on and know it quickly.

'Morale is especially important. I want you to move about among the troops and report to me everything you see, hear and feel.'

It was a delicate assignment and, in that country, a fairly tough one, but it was valuable experience for the work that Holmes was later called upon to do: the provision of absolutely accurate information. He came under fire for the first time and discovered what no training exercise could teach: the presence of a real enemy, the urgency of operations, the constant preparedness, the frequent improvisations. He found that 2nd/1st Punjab were here in Mayforce, in Hunt's 55th Brigade, and thought it ironical that he could not now join them.

Units were often difficult to locate in the roadless country and Holmes found that the best way to get about was on horseback, using a mount lent him by a company operating the mule trains. He rode pretty hard every day, leaving his horse in someone's charge whenever he had to go forward on foot. When he had to cross some stretch of water he would commandeer a sampan and sometimes had to enforce obedience on the boatman at the point of the pistol.

The country was extraordinarily empty and unfriendly and he was often oppressed by a sense of loneliness, a feeling to which he would be much accustomed in the future. For the first time he encountered a local population which, if not actually hostile, was aloof, avoiding contact with our troops. They were silent as he passed. No salaams. No smiles. Particularly in the half-empty Buthidaung, where he met no one but Mughs. Evidently, he thought, they believe that we shall be pulling out and so they had better not be too friendly, for fear of being denounced by their local enemies when the Japs arrived. The experience taught him, as a lesson for the future, how important it was to gain the confidence and friendship of the local population.

More serious still, however, was the state of morale that he found in some of the British and Indian troops, including some of their officers. He spent an hour or two each day with the forward units and found that some were tired out and had lost the offensive spirit. He had to report to Curtis that one British battalion, tired from long action, was scamping its patrols. Worst of all was the discovery that a whole company of Sikhs had deserted during the night. Supplies were running short and rations had to be cut.

Fortunately, that was only part of the story. The Japanese were exerting strong pressure, constantly trying to cut in behind the British units, but Mayforce as a whole was well in hand. Holmes's own regiment was in good shape and he took particular pleasure in reporting to Curtis that 1st Lincolnshires, under P. H. Gates, were right on the top line and that, whenever he visited them, he felt that something positive was happening.

Then, in the second week of May, the mango showers having already begun and the villagers having started hastily to plough their paddy-fields, came Slim's order for the withdrawal of 26th Division to Cox's Bazar. Mayforce had already been dissolved and Holmes was ordered to join divisional headquarters. The very difficult withdrawal operations, which involved the convergence of widely dispersed units from several directions upon the bottle-neck of the rickety bridge at Bawli Bazar, was made in exemplary order under exceptionally able staff planning. The infantry and other units marched by night, leaving the poor tracks clear for transport by day. Divisional headquarters crossed the quivering bridge in a tremendous down-pour. Holmes marched with some old Punjab friends, very wet but in good fettle. He was gradually being broken in.

The Japanese, as anxious as their enemies to get into monsoon quarters, did not attempt to follow up, but settled down to build their 'Golden Fortress' in that fierce country north of the tunnels road that we have briefly noticed.

3
V Force

Among those at 26th Division headquarters was a Japanese-speaking Intelligence officer who had been posted for the express purpose of interrogating prisoners. He found, however, that there was none to interrogate. Talking to Denis Holmes, he remarked that the only chance he could see of getting any was through V Force.

Holmes had occasionally heard of this organization, but only in a vague sort of way; people seemed to think it was a very amateurish outfit. He asked, 'Just what is this V Force?'

The Intelligence officer proceeded to explain.

Burma, he said, had from the beginning lacked any military organization fit to take the field as a modern army. In particular it had lacked an Intelligence Service. The Japanese, on the other hand, had been preparing for the invasion for a long time. There had been some 32,000 Japanese in Burma before the war, nearly all of them spies. They knew virtually every jungle track in the country, many of which were marked in advance for them. Among the most active agents whom they procured were the yellow-robed Buddhist monks (*hpoongyis*), who, on more than one occasion, had treacherously led British and Indian troops into prepared ambushes, where they were butchered in the most barbarous manner. Of course, there were plenty of friendly and loyal Burmese and some were serving as soldiers, but, because of their hatred of Indians and their consequent dislike of the British, who were friends of the Indians, many of the Arakanese Mughs and nearly all *hpoongyis* were pro-Japanese.[1]

---

[1] Of course, there were many exceptions, notably the charming and cultured Colonel Shwe Zan, who became the commanding medical officer of 26th Division.

In the Arakan campaign just concluded Lloyd had suffered in much the same way as Alexander and Slim had done in the Great Retreat, and something must be done, the Intelligence officer said, to create a service that would keep us informed of enemy movements. Several clandestine outfits had been created for this purpose – Force 136, Z Force and so on, without any co-operation between them – but the one that interested him most, because it worked just behind the enemy front lines, was V Force.

Created just before the end of the Retreat, V Force had originally been intended by Wavell as armed native guerrillas to harass the enemy's lines of communication, should he invade Indian territory. That had never happened, but the force had done fine service in helping forward the 400,000 refugees, Indian, British and Burmese, who had poured in from the south under the most harrowing conditions.

It had all begun in the main, central front in Manipur and along the Assam border, where V Force had a strong military flavour, having been based on an armed gendarmerie known as the Assam Rifles.

Holmes broke in: 'Oh, I know them. I was seconded to them for a couple of years.'

A good outfit, the Intelligence man commented, but went on to say that it was quite different here. What was called the 'Arakan Zone' of V Force was a very unmilitary affair. It had not been formed until September 1942 in preparation for 14th Division's offensive, but, being composed of native villagers quite unsuited to the use of arms, had proved futile. The only bright spot in their dismal story had been a fine raid on Taung Bazar by a hell of a fine guy named Gretton Foster. General Lloyd had disbanded them in disgust but Slim, seeing their potential value in a purely Intelligence capacity, had stepped in to save them and General Lomax also was now giving them encouragement. Apart from two or three British officers, they were a civilian show, run by the shrunken remnants of the Burma Civil Service. 'I believe', said the Intelligence officer, 'that they are a man short.'

Holmes pricked up his ears; this sounded exciting. Like many another officer, he had a *penchant* for a lone mission and for a canoe of his own to paddle. Tired of hanging around divisional headquarters, he saw ahead several months of footling duties, living in a basha that leaked in the incessant rain. He wanted to be up and doing something. There was a serious and widespread rice famine and the thousands of sick and starving Indian refugees still pouring in from Burma, many of them dying at the roadside, made Cox's Bazar a melancholy place.

Accordingly he got permission to go forward to Bawli Bazar for an interview with the V Force commander. Crossing the rickety bridge in torrential rain, he found himself at the tin-roofed school, which now housed two officials of the Burma civilian administration, who had been given military rank to protect their statuses in an area dominated by soldiers.

The first of these was a very live wire with a most infectious laugh, named Denis Phelips. He was Deputy Commissioner for the District of Burma that included the Mayu Peninsula and had the acting rank of brigadier. The other was Lt-Colonel Archie Donald, known as 'Rockbound' Donald for some reason, a senior officer of the Burma police, a man of massive frame, hard living, jovial, and renowned for his 'good, mouth-filling oaths'. He was the one directly in charge of V Force on the Arakan front, under the general direction of Brigadier Marindin at Army Headquarters.

Over luncheon, at which Holmes, who was fond of his food, had 'the best chicken curry of my life', Donald explained the situation and went on:

'We have got some good men on the eastern side of the Mayu Range. Just the other side we've Anthony Irwin – son of the general, you know – with "Pirate" Edwards and John Salmon, and away in the Kaladan valley there is Gretton Foster. But it happens that we've no one now on the west side. Frank Bullen has gone down with a bad go of dysentery and can't be back for months. We must have someone quickly to take his place.'

He looked at Holmes quizzically, wondering how the latter was going to take it.

'We must be fair,' he continued, 'and tell you frankly from the start that this is a damned risky game. If you should get caught by those foul Japanese bastards, God help you.'

He let this sink in for a moment and went on:

'If you join us, you will be quite on your own. Some of the chaps you will have to deal with are a pretty rum lot, I can tell you. Jail-birds, smugglers, racketeers and all sorts. But some damned good types too. They are not soldiers and are not armed. You have got to use these chaps to gather in as much as you can about the enemy, his movements, supplies, unit identifications and so on.

'You must assess the validity of the information that you get and pass it back as quickly as possible. You have to learn whom you can trust and whom you can't and you have to look out for the double agent. But the chaps we use are nearly all Chittagonians, who loathe the Mughs and the Japs like hell, so are usually to be trusted. A lot depends on how they like you, but, as you speak Urdu and are used to Indian peasant types, you ought to get along.'

Holmes asked how they were organized and Donald replied:

'"Organized" is rather too fancy a word, but basically we have a "section" of five or six chaps in each village. We call these blokes "scouts". You'd have a few, plus some interpreters, at your headquarters, but otherwise the scouts are out in the villages on the enemy side or on the fringes of ours. They are on our regular payroll. They come in regularly to report to you and you meet them when you visit the villages yourself. When you have a special job for one of them you send someone from your camp with a message to the scout to meet you somewhere.'

Holmes asked: 'What sorts of chaps are these scouts, sir?'

'Oh, odds and sods of all kinds. Humble types, you know. Most of them pretty decent blokes, with plenty of guts. Others have police records and would cut your throat for five bob, but they know we have the edge on them.'

Holmes laughed and the big policeman went on:

'Then, usually much farther in behind the Jap lines, we have a number of "agents", acting individually. They are men of higher intelligence and more responsible status. Their information can be important and we pay them well, but they have to be bloody careful, otherwise the Jap 'll pin them to the ground with bayonets and skin them alive. We suspect some of them of being double agents.'

Somewhat sarcastically, Holmes said:

'Sounds fascinating, sir. Are these the only sources of information?'

'Oh no. You'd get plenty of reports, good or bad, from what we distinguish as "informers". They're people who come forward voluntarily with information. When our troops are doing well they roll up in dozens; when we take a knock they dry up. You can't accept all they say, of course, and you've got to put them through the hoop, like we coppers do, by close questioning.'

Holmes was enjoying Rockbound's racy narrative and he listened keenly as the big man went on:

'There are two other types that you would have to know about if you are rash enough to sign up with us. One is an outfit of rather special, long-range wallahs, deep in the country, run by Colonel Orr; most of them are known double agents and they are not your concern but you may be required to help them on occasions. The other is the Burma Intelligence Corps, a uniformed, army crowd, all Burmese, useful chaps, especially as interpreters, working on our side of the line, but they don't speak Bengali and so we sometimes have to work with them.'

Over a final drink, Donald asked:

'Well, what do you think?'

Holmes, listening to the rain cannonading on the tin roof, hesitated only a moment. This would not be soldiering as he knew it. No fighting. But it was something positive, something active and useful. Better than being a dog's-body at Div. HQ. Moreover, he would be running a show of his own. So he replied simply:

'When do I start, sir?'

As they parted soon afterwards on the dripping veranda, Phelips said: 'For God's sake, don't get captured, my dear fellow.' Holmes made a light-hearted reply and mounted his truck. Donald gave him a guide in the person of his interpreter, a ragged, shifty-eyed fellow whose native name was aptly anglicized as 'Dick Turpin'. He was a typical police informer, not at all a prepossessing herald to Holmes's new mission, but one who was quite representative of the strange new circle he was about to enter.

After another wet journey through the rain-sodden land,

Dick Turpin conducted him to a small basha in the forward defended localities a few miles south of Bawli. Here he found a very good Chittagonian cook named Danu Meah, who obviously became 'Danny', an interpreter named Shaffi – a little, clerkly fellow – and three or four hangers-on, the first of whom was Kaloo the Killer.

This oddly likeable rascal proudly confessed to having been the assassinator of the former Deputy Commissioner of Akyab, but, a fugitive from justice, he had to be wary of his movements. Besides being a killer, he was an expert thief. Aptly enough, Kaloo was conspicuous for the bright red staining of his lips by constant chewing of betel-nuts. At first Holmes thoroughly mistrusted him. How, he asked himself, can I rely on a chap with his record? Will he bump me off too? It was a chance that he had to take, but in course of time he found that Kaloo was not only entirely loyal to the British but was also a daring scout, a very good guide, a reliable contact with the villagers and very useful for interrogating people who would not have talked freely to anyone else: the shady, the cautious, the frightened.

Entirely different from Kaloo the Killer was a queer-looking bird named Abdul Khalique, but more often referred to ironically as 'the Inspector'. On first meeting him Holmes could scarcely refrain from bursting into laughter at the man's comical appearance. His grey goatee beard and his serious mien – like Shakespeare's 'grave and reverend signiors' – contrasted ludicrously with his wardrobe, which consisted of a large topee, a *lungyi* or sometimes shorts, socks held up by suspenders, brown Japanese boots and a brown belt into which two and sometimes three pistols were menacingly thrust. Unlike Kaloo, he was the essence of respectability. The Mughs had murdered his family somewhere far beyond the Mayu country and his chief value was that he went about the villages urging support for the British cause. He and Kaloo had both served with V Force in the campaign just concluded.

Later on other scouts who were to be Holmes's companions in the adventures of the future came in one by one out of the rain – the sinister-looking *mulvi*, Muhammad Siddiq (who naturally became 'Sid Dick'), the fearless and eager Muhammad Shaffi, best of all the scouts, the shaggy 'Harpo Marx', the faithful 'Tommy-Gun' and 'Johnny' and others who will be encountered as the story unfolds. Several of them – strong, square-framed men – had the surname (as we should say) of 'Boli', which means a wrestler, the Chittagonians being very keen on that sport. Yakub Boli and Hashim Boli were later counted among the best. Many carried at the waist the traditional Burmese *dah*, a broad-bladed weapon, like a machete, excellent for cutting bamboo or chopping off the head of your enemy.

Left alone in this totally strange setting, Holmes felt completely at sea and utterly depressed. He did not know how to begin. From being a conventional soldier, an acolyte in an established hierarchy, a digit in a well-ordered system, in which chains of command, channels of communication, sources of supply, codes of behaviour were all nicely prescribed and the responsibilities apportioned, he felt as though he were an isolated particle flung off at a tangent into space by a revolving wheel. No one controlled his actions. Though he would be judged by his results, no one gave him any orders. He would have to make his own plans and devise his own methods. It would have been easy to do as little as possible.

Feeling again the loss of Khyber Khan, he ordered Danny to lay out his bedding roll in the basha, arranged his few possessions as tidily as possible and then went out for a chat with little Shaffi. Fortunately, everyone there spoke Urdu, which was the language of his own regiment.

His military training told him that his first task was to make a reconnaissance and, after very careful thought, he decided to do so in native dress, which, on Donald's advice, he had acquired at Bawli. He knew well the terrible penalty of being caught in such dress by the Japanese, but reflected that in uniform – even if only shorts and shirt – he would be spotted a long way off by enemy spies.

Accordingly he stripped off his khaki shorts and shirt and his boots and socks, and, with Shaffi's assistance, put on the Burmese *lungyi*, which is similar to the Malay *sarong*. It was a calf-length piece of cotton, of tartan design. The little interpreter showed him how to wrap it round his loins and tuck it in at the waist securely. He wore also a green vest and carried a green umbrella. He went barefoot. Beneath the lungyi he buckled on his webbing belt, in which his revolver was housed.

In this kit he felt extremely strange and conspicuous, his legs and arms very white, and he wondered whether he could get accustomed to walking about the country barefoot, though he had seen other British officers doing so, as the best means of avoiding the prevalent ailment of 'athlete's foot'. Shaffi reassured him, saying with a smile:

'You will pass, sahib. It is a pity that your hair is that mousy colour, but your legs and arms will soon get brown and your feet will harden. Barefoot is the best way in the monsoon mud. If you find it uncomfortable, you could wear gym shoes; several of our people do.

'But there is one more thing you must do, sahib. You must shave off your moustache. The Burmese are naturally smooth-faced people. Those that can grow any hair are cleanshaven until they are old men, and then they grow long beards.'

Holmes knew that Anthony Irwin and other V Force officers adopted the opposite course and grew beards, but he decided to follow Shaffi's advice and henceforth kept the whole of his face as smooth as possible. Putting a bold front on the world, bare-headed, barefoot and bare-faced, he sallied out under his green umbrella into the sodden land accompanied by Khalique, the 'Inspector'. He went first to the nearest village outside the British lines, but, finding it deserted of all but the rats and the flies, decided to go as far south as he could.

A great silence lay over the land, broken only by the cry of the barking deer, the flutter of the green pigeons and the parrots, the jabbering of monkeys, the rattle and the clatter of the swaying palm-leaves and the dense thickets of bamboo. He met no one on this first day, except for some starving and frightened Indian refugees. He spoke to them and told them that they had but a few more miles to go to meet friendly British troops.

The monsoon months were a period of inactivity in the forward zone of both armies. Some fifteen miles of sodden country separated the British forward defended localities from the outposts of the enemy's Golden Fortress. Accordingly, in this his first tour of duty with V Force, Holmes enjoyed no exciting experiences; but, although he could not know it at the time, the three wet months that he passed among the stilted villages, the flooded paddy-fields, the swollen chaungs, the groves of bamboos, the betel palms and the splendid mangoes were to be very valuable to him in the near future. It was his period of tutelage for a destiny not yet revealed. He got to know the people and their ways, became familiar with the sharp scents of the villages, compounded of ginger, onions and dried fish, drank tea with the headmen, strode among the small, scrabbling chickens, was struck by the brilliant dresses of the women and the scarlet lips of the betel-chewers, met and sized up many of his scouts, learnt to assess the value of the information that they brought him and how to classify it for credibility by the Intelligence staff at divisional and corps headquarters. Occasionally a suspected enemy agent was pulled in and sent back to Donald.

His most interesting encounters were with a few of the special agents who, on occasions, came out from behind the Japanese lines. Holmes found that they usually carried Japanese passports and were actually in Japanese service as spies or in some other way. 'Jacob', for example, was employed by the Japs as an interpreter and was found to have a good knowledge of enemy badges and organization and had been double-crossing them for months. Holmes was amused to find that sometimes the agents ran a profitable black market, carrying back British cigarettes, tea and cloth and selling them to the Japanese.

One of the most daring and most valuable was 'Rob Roy', who was a former public works contractor for the Burma Government and highly respected, but who had got himself some sort of official position with the Japanese. He was a small, sincere fellow, but justifiably very frightened, knowing that he was being watched by both the Japs and the Mughs. We shall see a good deal of 'Rob Roy' and of his home-town, the distant coastal village of Alethangyaw, where Holmes and his friends of the commandos and the West Africans were to participate in stirring deeds.

Thus, squelching through the mud, his face, hands and legs covered at evening with anti-mosquito cream, Holmes went about the dripping countryside as much as possible, usually under his umbrella, feeling very unmilitary and finding the variations in the village names most confusing. Khalique and Kaloo were his usual companions, each in his own way highly entertaining. In these months wetness was all. Their sodden lungyis flapped about their legs and to get any clothes dried was almost impossible. The whole countryside reeked of dampness. The Mayu hills were often totally obscured by the density of the rain, which, having descended, cascaded down the hillsides to create rushing torrents in the chaungs.

Everywhere Holmes encountered a silent fear of the Japanese and every man's suspicion of his neighbour. He very soon learnt that, even in the friendliest village, he was unwelcome at night. At first, as the sun began to set above the Bay of Bengal, he hoped that a headman would allow him to stay the night in his basha, but quickly took his cue when the headman politely said:

'You will be wishing to go home now, sahib, will you not?'

On such occasions he had either to make an eerie journey back to his basha in the torrential rain, or, if the night were fortunately dry, to curl up somewhere out in the open under the swarming mosquitoes and the magnificent canopy of the myriad stars.

Very soon, however, his men were bringing news of the Japanese activities in building their Golden Fortress, and he detailed one or two of his scouts to pass themselves off as coolies carrying bags of commandeered rice to enemy forward positions and others to watch enemy patrols north of Razabil.

As a result, he learnt that Razabil was being made into a formidable and well-concealed fortress, with fighting positions tunnelled into the hillside and that a redoubt was being built two and a half miles north of it, which, he saw, would also cover the approach to Maungdaw. This was at a waterside village called Hathipauk ('Elephant Gap').

As he himself went deeper into the country the sensation that there was no one in front of him but a dangerous enemy lent excitement to his life. He made special friends with the Naf fishermen and frequently got one of them to paddle him down the enemy-held coast in a kisti, going as near as he dared to Maungdaw, now in Japanese hands.

He quickly got accustomed to these primitive dug-out canoes, which he grew to prefer to other craft for his later clandestine trips in hostile waters. He would tie up in some chaung, make contact with his scouts there and return with the tide, watching the fish-hawks wheel overhead and the cormorants dive for their prey. He learnt that the Japanese held Maungdaw in only moderate strength and that they were not using it as a port. In July, when he learnt of the brilliant raid on Maungdaw carried out by his friends of the 1st Lincolnshires, under the leadership of the heroic Major Ferguson Hoey,[1] he regretted that he had had no part in it, the V Force officer who guided the Lincolnshires having been Captain Guinsberg, who had come across the river with them from Teknaf.

In this very odd and unnatural life, Holmes's greatest trial was not the physical discomfort of the monsoon, but loneliness. A gregarious man, he liked good company. He took frequent occasion to visit the nearest British troops and sometimes they would visit him, but night always brought on the sense of separation. He lay uneasily under a mosquito net in his basha, listening to the thudding of the rain, to the rasping cry of the nightjar, the demented shriek of the hoolock monkey and the howling of the jackals, while swarms of flying insects fluttered round his hurricane lamp, immolating themselves on its hot glass bowl. He read a great deal, particularly *The Seven Pillars of Wisdom* and the delightful books on Burma by Maurice Collis.

Yet, despite all the adversities – the loneliness, the everlasting rain and the absence of people of his own kind, a sense of magic in the situation began to steal over him, a sense that was to be multiplied ten times when he became involved in the stirring events of the next campaign.

When, on Bullen's return from sick leave in late September the end of his secondment to V Force came, Holmes accepted it with some regret. He feared that, on return to formal military duty, he might again be cast by fortune into some backwater of the war. Such, indeed, was nearly his fate, for, after having been sent on leave (which he spent at Bangalore), he was ordered to rejoin 26th Division headquarters, who had now been relieved by the newly arrived, keen-looking 7th Indian Division and who

---

[1] Seven months later Hoey, in death, won the Victoria Cross in an act of superlative gallantry.

were living in ease and comfort right back at Chittagong. There
he found that he was again what the army calls an 'odd file',
with no specific post. So it was with relief that he was given
another lone mission by the divisional administrative staff
officer, Lt-Colonel K. N. Cariappa (who later became C-in-C
of the Indian Army).

He was required to make a reconnaissance of the Sangu
River valley and eastward over the fierce Arakan Hill Tracts to
the valley of the Kaladan, in order to find a supply route for
mules and porters of the 81st West African Division, who were
to form a left flank guard for the next 'campaigning season'. It
was a wild, little-known and roadless country. The survey meant
first a long trip up the Sangu by dug-out canoe (during which
Holmes's fierce Pathan escort, Fazal, threatened to shoot the
Bengali boatmen when they grumbled about their food),
followed by a stiff climb on foot over the jungle-clad Arakan
Tracts. He reached the Kaladan valley and visited a lonely V
Force post near Daletme.

The reconnaissance occupied Holmes for about a fortnight.
Having returned to Chittagong about the end of October and
made his report, he began to grow restive again. Lomax's
division was still kicking its heels in reserve. The new campaigning season was fast approaching and he asked himself:

'How can I get back into the war? Am I going to get side-
tracked again?'

He was overjoyed, therefore, to learn of the arrival of advance
elements of the already celebrated 5th Indian Division, which
included two battalions of his 1st Punjab Regiment: the 1st
Battalion under the Australian, 'Digger' Morrison, and the 2nd
under the Irish W. G. Smith, which had done so well in First
Arakan but had now been transferred to 5th Division. Smith's
adjutant, Captain Gordon Howe, an able officer of charming
personality, was a great friend of Holmes. Holmes immediately
made his way to divisional headquarters and secured a posting
to the 2nd Battalion; but soon afterwards he was recalled and
told by Lt-Colonel Freddy Noble, chief staff officer of the
division, that Rockbound Donald had asked for his return to
V Force. Was Holmes willing to go?

Holmes was in two minds. He had the choice between two

desirable things: service in the line with his own regiment or what amounted to an independent command. The memory came back to him of the days of 'magic' and he said 'Yes.'

He was taken in to see the divisional commander, Major-General Harold Briggs, commonly known as 'Briggo', and beheld a square, calm, matter-of-fact officer who eyed him keenly and said:

'I understand that you want to rejoin the V Force and that your CO has agreed to release you?'

Holmes assented and Briggs went on:

'V Force can be very useful to me if it can send me back accurate and timely information about the Japs. It is up to you to make it a success or otherwise. I shall be keeping an eye on these things personally and if you can produce the goods you shall have every possible backing from my staff; if not, you will have to make way for someone else.'

He asked a few searching questions and dismissed Holmes with wishes for his success.

Holmes came away feeling as though he had drunk a delicious tonic, for Briggs had a great gift of inspiring confidence. Holmes was to meet him several times during the forthcoming operations and always found him ready to go out of his way to help and encourage. Holmes now once more made forward to Bawli for a talk with Donald.

He sensed a new atmosphere everywhere. Something was clearly in the wind. Things were now more orderly. The roads were a little better. The bridge had apparently been rebuilt and was well maintained. Above all, however, was the tremendous uplift in the bearing of the troops of both the new divisions. He had never before seen such fit and confident men. They were dressed in the new jungle-green battle dress, with long sleeves, trousers instead of shorts and wide-brimmed felt hats of Australian style. They looked, Holmes thought, thoroughly workmanlike and absolutely crackerjack. He noticed a sprinkling of medal ribbons of the right sorts, which showed that many of the units had been tested and proved in battle. The 5th, their shoulders adorned by the red 'ball of fire' badge that gave the division its popular name, shone also with the halo of distinguished service in the Western Desert. The 7th, the Golden

Arrow Division, had not yet won any halo, but there was a freshness and keenness in its bearing and it was commanded by the audacious 'spearhead general' Frank Messervy, another soldier of fame in both the Desert and Abyssinia. Briggs and Messervy were both very much front-line generals – in Messervy's case several times too much so!

It was in the sparkling atmosphere generated by these new arrivals that Denis Holmes entered upon his second and most stirring secondment to V Force. Rockbound Donald, in his robust idiom, told him at their interview that Frank Bullen had been transferred to other duties and Holmes was to take his place on a more permanent basis; his terrain, as before, was to be the west side of the Mayu hills and he was to work with 5th Division.

He was not to base himself in that territory, however, but at the small town of Teknaf, situated on the opposite shore of the River Naf, where a narrow tongue of land, inexactly called the Teknaf Peninsula, juts out into the Bay of Bengal.

Holmes was a good deal surprised, for Teknaf, which was in Indian territory, seemed well away from the war that he wanted to be in. It was separated from the Mayu Peninsula by two miles of water plus a great deal of mud. He said to Donald:

'Sounds as if you are sending me off to a backwater, sir.'

'You'll find it's a jolly lively backwater, Watson,' replied the big policeman, and told him why.

Meanwhile, all through the monsoon months, the rival armies had both been hatching their plots for the coming campaign season of 1943/44. Each knew that the other was preparing for an offensive. Each had been considerably reinforced and each was now operating under a new command structure.

The Japanese main plan was strongly influenced by Wingate's First Chindit operation, which had shown that British troops could penetrate deep into their territory. The enemy Commander-in-Chief accordingly decided to forestall any offensive by the British 4th Corps on the main, central sector by attacking first, wiping out 4th Corps in the Imphal area by swift, encircling movements and establishing his forces on the massive mountain barrier along the border of India proper, where he would have an almost impregnable position. The enemy's code name for this main offensive was *U-Go*.

An integral and vital part of it was that it should be preceded by a diversionary one in Arakan under the code name *Ha-Go*. This was intended to threaten to turn the British right flank by an advance into the plains of Bengal and Assam and thereby, be it noted, to force the British commander into committing his reserves. This Arakan offensive, from the firm base of the Golden Fortress, was entrusted to the severe, Prussian-faced General S. Sakurai, who had led the celebrated 33rd Division during the invasion of Burma with dramatic speed and aggression. The command in Arakan was elevated to the status of an Army (28th Army) and the division that we have specially to note is 55th Division, now led by the grim-visaged Lt-General Hanaya.

On the Allied side far-reaching changes had taken place by November. The young and brilliant figure of Lord Louis Mountbatten appeared, to take command of all Allied forces in South-Eastern Asia, where his critical decisions and personal influence were to have far-reaching effects. General Sir George Giffard was appointed to command all the land forces (11th Army Group), Bill Slim was promoted to command the new 14th Army, which in substance meant the British forces on the central and Arakan sectors, and Lt-General Philip Christison stepped into his shoes as Commander of 15th Corps in Arakan. Other new appointments were those of Wavell as Viceroy of India and of General Sir Claude Auchinleck, idol of the Indian Army, as C-in-C India, which did not include operational command on the Burma front, though his influence on training and morale was profound.

The Allied plan was based on what was known or conjectured of the enemy's. On the far left Stilwell's Chinese were to make another attempt at an offensive, assisted by a very large-scale airborne penetration by Wingate's Chindits. In the centre no attempt was yet to be made at a counter-invasion of Burma over the two frail tracks that led that way; instead 4th Corps was to draw back to the hill-girt Imphal plain, to await the attack of the enemy and defeat him on ground of its own choosing.

The opening move of the Allied campaign was to be made in Arakan, without foreknowledge of the impending *Ha-Go*. Christison was to launch an offensive for the recapture of the Mayu Peninsula with his two fine new divisions, and with 81st West African Division as his flank guard in the roadless Kaladan valley. He assigned 5th Division to the west of the mountain range and 7th to the rugged east. As a disagreeable surprise for the enemy, Christison had also been given a fine regiment of tanks in 25th Dragoons and their associated engineers and infantry. Commanded by Lt-Colonel H. R. C. Frink, and equipped with Lee-Grant tanks, it was part of the new armoured force that had been created on Slim's insistence and by the drive of Colonel 'Atty' Persse and was to prove its worth on a memorable day.

Of no less significance was the fact that, by Mountbatten's pressure, the Allied air forces had at last been reinforced and the closest tactical co-operation between ground and air had been systematically worked out. It was to be manifested in a way in which it had never before been employed on any of the world's battlefields and which was to be Mountbatten's particular and outstanding innovation in the art of war.

4

At Dewdrop Inn

Second Arakan Begins – Into Enemy Country

Holmes's assignment to Teknaf marks the beginning of a period
where the story gathers pace and events crowd upon one another
rapidly in an ever-changing scene. Daring reconnaissances,
armed raids on enemy positions, rescues and attempted rescues
became, after a little while, almost nightly occurrences; for
nearly all these operations had to be launched in the dark.

It was now that Holmes found the value of his former secondment to V Force. His novitiate had been completed and its
lessons learnt methodically without heroics. He returned a
qualified practitioner, knowing how to set about a problem;
knowing, above all, the importance of making friends with
people of all sorts, understanding their ways, gaining their
trust and never letting them down.

He knew how to move about the country unobtrusively and
had expanded his knowledge of tongues. The great difference
was that formerly his scouting had been almost wholly confined
to land, but now nearly every operation was to be a seaborne
one, carried out usually in one of the little kistis to which he had
taken a fancy before, but sometimes in the roomier, carvel-
built sampan, propelled by two oars astern and protected against
the perils of the deep by an eye painted on the prow; occasionally larger craft were used.

He grew very fond of the sea and the seashore, enjoying its
'exquisite loneliness', the freshness and invigoration of its air, the
absence of dust, flies and mosquitoes and discovering a sense of
freedom and independence. Curiously, he found in the sea also
a feeling of superiority over the enemy for, whatever the

Japanese might do on land, they never attempted to govern the
waves, except by the fire of some small, land-based field guns,
so that the small British ships and the still smaller craft of the
Chittagonians roamed the waters unchallenged.

Arriving at Teknaf, Holmes found a busy little coastal town
with a jetty. His accommodation, in contrast to his former
humble abode, was a large and commodious basha nicely
suited to the uses of a soft life. He had only a tiny staff, consisting
of Muhammad Yusuf, the interpreter, a Mugh cook and a few
itinerant scouts, including the courageous 'Burke' and 'Hare'
(nicknamed after two notorious murderers of the 1820s), who
were responsible for watching the coastline south of Teknaf and
who several times rescued crashed RAF pilots or salvaged their
machines. The Teknaf Peninsula was garrisoned by British
troops, as a precaution against the possibility of an enemy landing, and Holmes's gregarious instincts responded to their
cheerful company. After a week or two he found that his basha
had become a favourite port of call not only for their officers but
also for the numerous visitors of all conditions that came to
Teknaf, including General Briggs. He welcomed all to 'drop in'
and so caused a board to be painted with the sign DEWDROP
INN and nailed it up over the basha.

Except for the muddy eastern shore, fringed all the way
upriver with forbidding mangrove swamps, the peninsula had
an oriental allure, the forest-clad hills that formed its spine
roamed by wild elephants and dotted with pagodas and the
plain enlivened by flocks of red and green parakeets busily
flying between the wooded foothills and the paddy-fields.

Very different, however, were the inhabitants. Teknaf itself
was a nest of spies, rumour-mongers and doubtful characters of
all sorts, including a great many Mughs. Even before the war it
had been notorious for smuggling, dope trafficking and other
rackets. Many of the Teknaf population, including virtually all
the police, were known or suspected fifth columnists. One of
Holmes's tasks was to keep an eye on these gentry, interrogate
suspicious new arrivals, watch for any political agitators trying
to get into India from the other side of the Naf, patrol the coast
and provide guides for military patrols. A few arrests were made
but Holmes was not interested in this kind of police work.

What interested him most was the distant, mysterious shore beyond the Naf, flanked with oozy mud and dark thickets of mangrove or with the massive forms of mangoes and the leaning clusters of palms that gave notice of human habitation; and, beyond all, the serrated crest of the Mayu hills draped with a curtain of black jungle or exposing their perpendicular flanks in rose-pink rock. All that enemy flank, he knew, was held by one of the best Japanese formations, the 112th Brigade, commanded by the redoubtable Tanahashi, who had led the audacious break-in on the British 6th Brigade in First Arakan.

Looking eastwards to this hostile shore from Dewdrop Inn, Holmes and his visitors experienced that mixture of sensations which the perceptive soldier undergoes on contemplating enemy country: wonder, expectancy, a fierce covetousness, and a proper apprehension of the unknown. In that terrain, unseen, are quantities of men who are your deadly enemies. What mischief are they up to? How can you kick them out and possess the land yourself?

It was his business to find out what they were up to. Much evidence was brought in to him across the water by his scouts, but as often as he could he hired a kisti from the local fishermen and, wearing again the lungyi and travelling barefoot, he paddled upriver by night through the flickering phosphorescence and the slithering jellyfish to the village of Wabyin on the eastern bank of the Naf. Not far from there and about a mile from the enemy outposts, V Force had a small, well-concealed basha.

At Wabyin he met again the old gang from his first secondment, including the red-lipped Kaloo the Killer and the comic-opera 'Inspector' Khalique. He met also some very significant new ones. Outstanding among these was another Shaffi – Muhammad Shaffi – totally different from the little interpreter. Muhammad Shaffi came into the little hut early one morning and Holmes beheld a fine-looking, broad-shouldered, young fellow in his middle twenties with an infectious smile, wearing a khaki vest and carrying a pistol in his lungyi. Holmes summed him up at once as a born guerrilla fighter. He soon discovered that Muhammad Shaffi was a natural leader, absolutely fearless and burning with ambition to kill the 'yellow dogs'. In peacetime he was a farmer, of a good family, respected for their upright character.

On the many expeditions that they were to make together it was always Shaffi who instinctively took the van, whether in a canoe or afoot. He had an inborn instinct to take charge and Holmes readily acquiesced, for not only did Shaffi know the Mayu countryside well but also had the sharp and sensitive perceptions of a wild animal. He had more eyes than six ordinary men, acute hearing and, more remarkable still, a nose so sensitive that it could discern that peculiar, sickly-sweet smell of Japanese soldiers twenty-five yards away.

After their second or third raid together, Holmes asked him: 'Why are you never afraid, Shaffi? Why do you always go in front?'

'Allah is generous,' replied the young Muslim. 'A man can die only once. You pray and I pray and I am sure God has given more than one life to each of us.'

This Muslim fatalism was typical of Holmes's Chittagonians. In his Christian way, he had somewhat similar views, believing in the Afterlife and sharing the comforting philosophy of the British soldier that if an enemy shell did not have your regimental number on it, you were safe. His scouts noted that he carried a rosary and often observed him at his private devotions and such evidence of faith in a common God and of belief in 'the evidence of things not seen' created a bond between them.

It was in keeping with Shaffi's instinct for leadership that he also constituted himself Holmes's protector. He had a fervent admiration for everything British, a word that he used on every possible occasion. So high was Shaffi's reputation and esteem in that strangely mixed little company that he was honorifically given the Indian Army title of Jemadar.[1] Holmes did not, however, address him as 'jemadar sahib' as one would the genuine article in the Indian Army, but simply as 'Shaffi'.

Second in standing and value to the jemadar but totally different from him, was Muhammad Siddiq, or 'Sid Dick'. As we have briefly noted before, he was a *mulvi*, a Muslim religious teacher, and wore a black beard and a white skull-cap. He had a

[1] One of the several ranks of Viceroy's Commission Officers. (See Appendix A.)

somewhat severe and dictatorial manner and a rather sinister, Rasputin-like face, with piercing black eyes, but, by reason of his status, commanded great respect. Siddiq could quote long passages from the Koran by heart and every Friday he called the Muslims to prayer. He knew the Mayu Peninsula like the back of his hand and would go anywhere with confidence, unsuspected of having any military purpose. His favourite pastime was cutting Japanese telephone lines.

A third man was an amusing and innocent-looking fellow who lived on his wits, named Yakub Boli, one of the wrestlers, strongly built but past his prime, wearing grey side-whiskers. He was a valuable and brave man, travelling the whole peninsula right down to Akyab. He was always anxious for supplies of sugar, tea and cigarettes to sell to the Japs. It was a time when British and Indian troops were issued with a particularly noxious weed called the V cigarette, made in India. On their first meeting Yakub said to Holmes;

'Sahib, I don't want any more of those filthy V cigarettes. Even the Japanese can't stand them. They spoil my reputation. You must bring me Gold Flake or Players, please.' Holmes mistrusted him at first, but found him sturdy and loyal.

It was on his return to Dewdrop Inn after one of his trips across the water that Holmes was surprised and delighted to find the stalwart form of his old orderly, Khyber Khan, waiting for him at the steps. The faithful sepoy, after having been pushed from one transit camp to another, even right back to the regimental depot far away at Jhelum, 1,400 miles away on the Kashmir border, had doggedly persisted in his hunt for his master, following one false clue after another for nearly eight months. And never once had he been separated from Holmes's old bedding roll, which he now dutifully returned. Holmes was deeply touched by this wonderful example of fidelity and said: 'You shall be my staff NCO now, Khyber, and so I will give you three stripes.'

'You mean I am to be a havildar, sahib?'

'That's right, Khyber.'

'Thank you, sahib; I hope I shall get the pay, too.'

'I'm afraid you won't get it from the Government but I shall see that you are properly paid.'

'Very well, sahib, I shall now take charge here and see that you are properly looked after. You will need a Bren-gunner, too. Also, I shall have to teach these stupid people here how to handle weapons. Already I find they have no idea about rifles even. How can you trust such people?' For, as a member of an Indian warrior hill-tribe, Khyber had a lordly contempt for the Bengali plainsmen.

Second Arakan Begins

Meanwhile Holmes had also been keeping in close touch with 5th Division. The monsoon was over, though there would still be the occasional damaging downpour.

Christison's corps, supported by 224 Group, RAF, was off its mark on time on the operation to be known as 'Second Arakan'. His plan was first to capture the two formidable buttresses of the Golden Fortress – Razabil on the western side of the Mayu Range and Letwedet on the eastern – then to seize the tunnel entrance and isolate and reduce the main fortress. On 19 September Frank Messervy took command of both sectors, but when 5th Division had eased in, Briggs took over the western sector on 9 November. Holmes watched 5th Division begin its advance from Bawli Bazar and kept close contact with it. Very soon, instead of reporting to Donald, as he had done before, he was reporting direct to Briggs's staff and became virtually part of the division, an arrangement entirely to his liking and bringing him in intimate contact with operations.

As the division advanced the primitive road from Bawli was improved, bridges were built over the numerous chaungs, which were crowded with sampans provided by V Force, and a very busy traffic began to flow both ways of light vehicles, ambulances, mules and artillery. Instead of rain, there were huge clouds of choking dust, stirred up by wheel and hoof. Of a dirty yellow-grey, it obscured the sun and the Mayu hills, thickly coated all vegetation, buildings, animals and the human body and became a sore affliction to everyone.

By 19 November 5th Division had driven in the enemy outposts and were five miles from Maungdaw and the adjacent fortress of Razabil. In front of them now was the redoubt near

'Elephant Gap' (Hathipauk). Things were getting warm. The artillery fire could plainly be heard at Teknaf. The heat was building up for the major battle, in which one of the great prizes was the port of Maungdaw for, primitive though its facilities were, its possession would resolve the infuriating problems of Christison's tortuous lines of communication with India. Furthermore, Maungdaw had become a symbol. Its recapture would constitute that victory – that very first victory in the Burman campaign – which Britain and India, and Winston Churchill particularly, so keenly wanted for the restoration of morale and prestige.

A little later Holmes learnt that, on the other side of the hills, Messervy's division, by a brilliant circuitous manœuvre, had assaulted and captured another redoubt and driven the enemy smartly from the adjacent range of hills in their first serious fighting. A good beginning. Meanwhile the 81st West African Division, without transport and carrying their loads on their heads, as was their wont in their own lands, had reached their flanking position in the Kaladan Valley and had begun their hard mission on foot.

Into Enemy Country

Things were warming up for V Force also. Information from Holmes's scouts across the water was coming in fast. Just after Christmas one of them brought him word that an important agent, named 'Baba Khan' for security reasons, who lived in the country south of Maungdaw, had some important information for him; could the major sahib arrange to meet him?

Baba Khan, an educated man of good standing and son of the headman of the important village of Godusara, had a contract to supply rice to the Japanese and was therefore well placed to report their troop movements and locations. Among these enemy units, here as elsewhere along the front, was a traitor army of Indians raised by the Japs and euphemistically called the 'Indian National Army'. They were completely useless as soldiers and were contemptuously referred to by Slim's troops as 'Jiffs'. Now it happened that, under threat of torture, Baba Khan had been forced to give his teen-age daughter to a Jiff

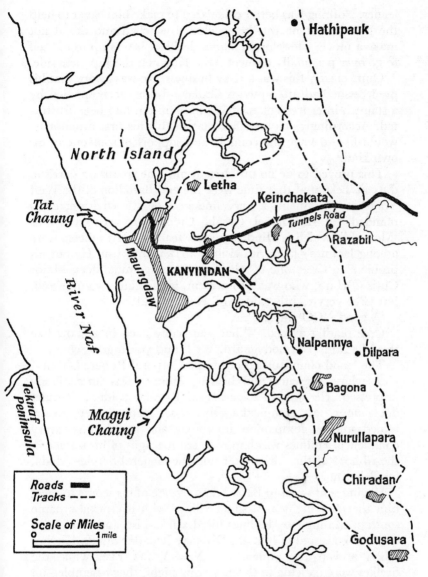

Fig. 3. The Maungdaw scene. Outlines as at low tide, when most of coast line is a broad belt of mud. At high water parts of the coast become islands.

leader. Nothing was better calculated to make him eager to help the British, but he was being closely watched and dared not make a move. Therefore, Holmes decided, it was up to himself to go over personally to meet Baba Khan on the Japanese side.

Quite clearly this was a risky business. He was aware that his predecessor had attempted a similar mission, accompanied by a staunch interpreter named Waji Ullah, but had been frustrated. Accordingly, Holmes felt that in this his first attempt he would like to have the comfort and support of someone of his own kind.

This proved to be no problem at all. The troops on garrison duty at Teknaf at that time were the 2nd Battalion of the West Yorkshire Regiment, a very fine unit of 5th Division, commanded by Lt-Colonel Gerald Cree, who was known as 'Moonshi', which is Hindustani for 'teacher'. His officers were among Holmes's favourite visitors at Dewdrop Inn. He put his problem to Cree, one of whose company commanders, Major Chris O'Hara, who was also present, immediately volunteered, but Cree very rightly said 'No.' Holmes said:

'A good NCO will do, sir.'

Cree readily agreed. 'What you really need in a show like this,' he said, 'is a bodyguard. We'll find you a good chap.'

The 'good chap' turned out to be Corporal Robert Disbury, with whose presence and bearing Holmes was immediately impressed. He was an experienced Regular soldier, of quiet demeanour, fair complexion, square-set features, very determined and a companion in whom one could have every confidence. Holmes was happy to see the signs of his service in the ribbons of the Africa Star and the General Service Medal for Palestine.

Having sent word to Baba Khan by one of his scouts to meet him the next night at a small village with a crackjaw name south of Maungdaw, Holmes hired a fleet kisti and briefed his team. It consisted of himself, Disbury, Jemadar Shaffi, Khyber Khan and two boatmen. On New Year's Eve, while the fireflies were dancing in the gathering night, they assembled on the beach and embarked in the kisti. All wore the lungyi. With his inborn instinct to lead, the jemadar stationed himself in the prow. The beach, still warm from the day's sun, was muted to the colour of pearls. The night was cold, with a sharp, damp breeze. A brilliant canopy of stars glittered in the sky.

At the turn of the tide they slipped out quietly. The small waves lapped gently against the hull of the canoe as the paddles dipped and rose. As their eyes became accustomed to the darkness, the six men could discern, against the lavender-grey of the farther distance, the densely black jungle of the Mayu hills.

Holmes, summarizing his orders again, ended by saying: 'Remember that we are not out to kill Japs. This is not a fighting mission. We fight only if attacked. So the first rule is absolute quiet. Until we meet our friends we must not be heard or seen.'

By 11 o'clock they were across the river on a still rising tide and were gliding into the big chaung called the Magyi ('Large Woman'), about a mile south of Maungdaw. Everything was quiet. No sign of activity ashore. A few silent strokes of the paddles took the canoe into a mangrove swamp on the south side. Here it was pitch black and Holmes felt that they were securely hidden.

He began to make preparations for landing in the oozy mud when a flare, of a type that Holmes had not seen before, suddenly shot up about a hundred yards away. In a moment other flares were shooting up on every side, one after another. Many of them seemed to be huge torches of dried grass. Sea and land were laid bare and the shadows of trees quivered as the lights hung and wavered above. They had been spotted.

Holmes and his companions felt as though suddenly stripped naked. They crouched low in their kisti and 'froze'. A faint click sounded as Disbury cocked his tommy-gun. Two or three Japanese machine-guns somewhere crackled to life, firing on fixed lines. Challenges were shouted from the opposite bank. A rifle-shot was fired and a bullet kicked up a splash of water not far away.

The critical moment was saved by the bland presence of mind of Jemadar Shaffi in the prow. Seizing the bow paddle from the scout beside him, he ostentatiously swung the canoe into the open, stood up and hailed the figures on the shore in Bengali.

'We are fishermen,' he shouted. 'We have been brought in by the tide. We have come to the wrong place. Please don't shoot. . . . Peace be with you.'

Then turning to Holmes, he grinned widely and whispered: '*Japani* sentry wallah, sahib.'

'Well done, Shaffi,' Holmes answered. 'Pull out to sea again.'

Unmolested, they paddled out as the flares died down and half an hour later landed safely in a smaller chaung to the southward, seven miles behind the enemy lines. Here again there was good concealment by mangroves. Leaving Khyber to guard the boatmen, Holmes went cautiously ashore with Disbury and Shaffi. Absolute quiet was scarcely possible, for they had to cross a short stretch of slimy, sticky mud, which squelched and sucked at each step. In the middle of this slough Disbury's lungyi fell off. He stood for a moment comically barelegged, tommy-gun in hand, and broke out into a whispered volley of the choicest barrack-room rhetoric. Holmes could scarcely forbear from bursting out laughing. Shaffi smiled his silver smile and helped the corporal to re-tie the cloth more securely.

Climbing out of the chaung, they moved silently across half a mile of paddy land, now almost dry and the rice harvested. Everything was utterly quiet. Not a soul to be seen. With Shaffi leading, they cautiously crept into a small village. It seemed to be deserted, the stilted bashas shut and silent among the banana and papaya trees, the ubiquitous bamboos and the ghostly white flowers of the palms. The night was embalmed with the languorous scent of jasmin. No animals were to be seen. No dogs barked. The air of desertion was suspicious; it usually meant that the Japanese had occupied the village and turned the inhabitants out.

Beyond the village was a bamboo fence. They climbed it as quietly as possible and came to a lone pastoral hut. This was the rendezvous where Holmes was to meet Baba Khan. Shaffi went forward alone to make sure that it was empty and the others followed him.

Holmes was feeling tremendously excited, but not a little anxious. If they had been seen by a hostile native or by any of the Jiff patrols that roamed the villages and the coast, their case would have been perilous. Nor was it unlikely that some enemy agent was keeping tabs on Baba Khan. He was therefore grateful for the quiet and reassuring presence of the corporal. He realized that it was just on midnight and he whispered:

'They'll be singing "*Auld Lang Syne*" at home now, corporal.'

'Aye, sir,' answered Disbury, 'and with something warm inside them.'

The minutes dragged on, seeming interminable, but in due time Shaffi returned, bringing Baba Khan with him. They all went into the little hut and Baba Khan greeted the two Englishmen with emotion and with deference, clasping their outstretched hands fervently in both of his and bowing deeply, obviously moved by strong feelings. Holmes was touched and put his arms round Baba Khan's shoulders reassuringly, for he could see that the agent was also labouring under a keen apprehension of the dangerous moment.

While Disbury mounted guard, Baba Khan lit a small oil lamp and they all sat on the floor to study a map that he produced. He spoke mainly in Arakanese, having little Hindustani. He had just come from Akyab and brought a wealth of information. Holmes was tremendously pleased. Here was really important news and of very high classification. Baba Khan was obviously a keen and diligent observer, with eyes and ears wide open. His records of deliveries of rice showed clearly the pattern of the movements and strengths of the enemy units and his report on the comings and goings of Japanese troops, aircraft and river craft at Akyab was of great value. He related how they had organized a supply route up the Kalapanzin in huge, pole-driven sampans and their attempts to establish a civil administration.

Holmes listened even more attentively when Baba Khan went on to tell him that the local Japanese Intelligence officer, a Lieutenant Honu or Ono, was to harangue a meeting of the elders of all the villages in that area on the following day. He asked where the meeting was to be.

'At Lambaguna, major sahib.'

'Lambaguna! Do you know what time, Baba Khan?'

'At noon, sahib.'

Holmes knew Lambaguna ('The Long Village'), seven miles

farther south, to be a large and prosperous village and an important supply centre for the Japanese. He thought: By God! I'll damned well go there. But he kept the thought to himself.

First, however, the party had to make its way back to the boat while it was still dark. A quick cigarette, a handshake and they were on their way again. But not, this time, without incident, which Shaffi's presence of mind again saved from being an ugly one. Before they had cleared the village they were challenged, in an unmistakably Indian voice, by a tall, bearded man wrapped in a blanket. Holmes recognized him at once as a Sikh. 'Bloody Jiff,' he thought.

Shaffi, however, who was leading as before, answered in a casual and friendly manner and engaged the Jiff in conversation, though what he really wanted to do was to put a bullet in the traitor's guts, while the two British soldiers kept their distance. Holmes squatted on the ground, apparently unconcerned. Behind him he heard a slight movement as Disbury got his tommy-gun ready, but was grateful that the corporal did not panic. After a few minutes the Jiff passed on his way, muttering into his beard some imprecation against the British Army. This was just the sort of encounter that Holmes had feared.

There was no time to be lost. Daybreak would mean their ruin. They made such haste as was safe, regained the boat and pushed off. But this time, instead of paddling back to Teknaf, Holmes, to the surprise of the others, ordered a southward course again. As they paddled, he told his companions what he proposed to do.

He was going down to the obscure little island of Nahkaungdo, which means 'the Short-nosed Village' but which inevitably became anglicized as 'No-Can-Do', where there was a small detachment of V Force scouts whom he had not yet met. There the party was to break up. He and the jemadar would march to Lambaguna that morning to see and hear Lieutenant Honu and the remainder were to return to Teknaf in the kisti. He said to Disbury:

'Sorry I can't take you with me, corporal.'

'Just as you say, sir,' Disbury answered; 'but I'm quite ready to carry on if I can be useful.'

'I should certainly like your company, but I'm afraid that in daylight you'd be spotted at once. And you'd have to leave your tommy-gun behind anyhow.'

The only man not disappointed was the jemadar. All the way back from the village he had been feeling full of elation. He now felt very proud that Holmes had picked him for his companion and he said:

'Allah be praised, sahib, you have made me a very happy man.'

They reached No-Can-Do at daybreak. It was New Year's Day, 1944. No-Can-Do was a tiny place, an elongated island at high tide, but connected with the mainland at low water and the haunt of circling fish-hawks and statuesque cormorants. A small cluster of fishermen's bashas was perched among some trees. The beach here was shelving, so that landing was easy, with very good cover against enemy observation from the mainland. The insignificant little place struck Holmes at once as a perfect jumping-off point for secret missions and it was this first, chance visit of his that soon led to the choice of No-Can-Do as a regular base for raiding parties.

As was to be expected at that time of year, the dawn was very cold, with a wet, breast-high mist, but the fishermen gave their unexpected guests the warmest of welcomes. Very soon they put before them a handsome breakfast of curried fish and rice, followed by buttermilk and the brown, unrefined cane-sugar in solid form known as *jaggery* or *gur*. Then, after a rest and a smoke and having sent Disbury and Khyber Khan back to Teknaf, Holmes got under way for his walk to The Long Village.

There was, however, a change in his little team. Shaffi had strongly advised him to take one of the local scouts with them in place of Disbury and the automatic choice – indeed he insisted on appointing himself – was the leader of the local scouts. This was a tall, strong, young fellow, with long hair, named Habibullah. Only about seventeen years old, he was mad-keen and reminded Holmes of a young Apache brave. He attached himself closely to Holmes and never left his side and later on became one of his regular troopers.

As they left No-Can-Do by the causeway, the sun rose in

strength, dissipating the wet mist, and the morning soon became very hot. The falling dew clattered down like a rolling of drums. Holmes was feeling in schoolboy spirits, the fatigue of the night's expedition forgotten. He experienced a return of the old sense of 'magic', as of being in another world, which he had felt on his secondment and which was to possess him on all his future missions. But he was awake to the perils into which he was voluntarily walking. Accordingly he had left his tommy-gun with Khyber Khan and had given his face a dusky appearance by a thin smear of black camouflage cream, as used by troops on night operations. Like many of the locals, he was wearing a tattered khaki shirt above his lungyi, under which he carried a ·38 pistol.

He was now some fourteen miles inside the enemy lines, but took comfort in the fact that neither the Japanese nor the Mughs were likely to suspect that an Englishman might be so foolhardy as to venture so deep within their fortress. What worried him a little was his gait, and he tried to moderate its natural briskness to the slow, smooth, languorous tempo of the Orient.

Having gone about a mile and a half, the little party were soon following a well-used, sandy track, which was easy going for bare feet. It was not long before they began encountering other people, making their way towards Lambaguna, with a few bullock-carts. They made no attempt to avoid them deliberately, but Holmes did what he could to appear inconspicuous, walking with head down and shoulders bent, with Habibullah close beside him. He smiled inwardly when he noticed that his two faithful scouts stuck closer and closer to him. Like zealous nursemaids, he thought.

As they neared Lambaguna, the flow of people increased and Holmes's pulses quickened as he began to rub shoulders with them. Keeping close together, the three at last went boldly right into Lambaguna, which was a long, straggling, prosperous village, with many houses of superior quality, typically Muslim, embowered within their compounds of fine trees. Holmes noticed that every house had an air-raid shelter. Huge mangoes, of so dark a green as to appear almost black, gave to the place something of a cathedral air. Plenty of shade here, Holmes noted thankfully, for by now he was sweating from the heat. He avoided looking directly at people, but found it very difficult to put on a mask of indifference when he was inwardly tingling with excitement.

He was jerked into sudden attention when, as the party neared the market-place, he saw a scattering of Japanese soldiers among the crowd, their long rifles slung across their shoulders. He felt his two companions press close to him. Only with difficulty did he keep his gaze modestly lowered, but he was able to note with interest their cheap uniforms, their ill-kept weapons and their curious canvas boots with the big toe separated. What struck him even more was their peculiar sticky-sweet smell, of which he had heard and for which Shaffi had so keen a nose.

Holmes found it damned odd to be so near to his enemies (whom he had never seen before), and yet not be able to shoot them down. He felt his hackles rising and acted his part only with difficulty. The Japs were very alert and bore themselves to the inhabitants as conquerors. From their searching looks at everyone Holmes supposed that they were there to watch for suspicious characters before the arrival of Lieutenant Honu. Us, for example, he thought.

Arriving in the market-place well before noon, the party squatted unobtrusively in a hot and dusty corner, buzzing with flies. The air was heavy with the sharp market smells of ginger, chillis, tamarind, onions and dried fish and the ground offensively speckled with the red spittle of betel chewers. Holmes felt drowsy and would have welcomed a short sleep. Shaffi, noting his discomfort, said to him:

'It is not very nice for you here, sahib, and not very safe. I am going to take you to a friend's house.'

'That would be very acceptable, Shaffi, but I have got to see what happens when this Lieutenant Honu arrives.'

'I have thought of that, sahib. You will be able to see very well from my friend's house.'

Holmes readily acquiesced. The three went down a little side-street and Shaffi led them into a typical Muslim compound. Some of the family were on the lower, open floor and, after a word with Shaffi, the owner took them upstairs and into a room which gave a good view of the market-place and its surroundings. Here, leaving Holmes in company with Habibullah, Shaffi went off alone, to mingle with the crowd and listen to Honu.

It was not long before Honu appeared, with an escort of ten soldiers. Holmes had already gathered that he was by way of being his opposite number and that he was respected by the local people for his sense of justice and also because, it was said, he had been a student of Islam. Holmes saw a youngish, upstanding, clean-shaven man, of lighter skin than the local inhabitants. All eyes were immediately turned to him as he began to walk through the crowd.

Holmes watched fascinated. He felt as though he was witnessing some secret and forbidden play or as though he himself, unseen, was playing the disembodied lead in an improbable spy drama. Here he was, an ordinary regimental officer, playing a Somerset Maugham part deep in the enemy heart-land, prying into their secrets, his presence unsuspected. With the enemy prowling around him, he yet felt utterly safe and confident. He had never thought of himself as a spy, but, by God, he was! He chuckled quietly, feeling that he was one-up on the Japs and that he had nothing to fear from them.

Holmes expected to see Honu mount some sort of dais and harangue the crowd, but, instead, he saw him walk up and down among them, stand still to address those around him, then walk on farther into the crowd and repeat his address, gesticulating the while. He spoke apparently in Urdu in a sharp, nasal voice. A pale, thin man with shaven head gave a Bengali interpretation in a flat monotone. Honu never came near enough for Holmes to hear distinctly what he said, but his main purpose, which Shaffi was able to amplify later, was to tell the people that they had nothing to fear as long as they kept the Japanese soldiers well supplied with rice and other provisions.

Otherwise his discourse was mainly a pep-talk. He urged them all to have faith in the 'Greater Asia Co-prosperity Sphere' (the bogus image set up by the Japanese to coin favour) and to have nothing to do with the White Man, who had now been driven out of nearly the whole of Asia. 'We know,' he said, 'that there are some evil men about who are in the pay of the British as spies. Have nothing to do with them. Report them to us. We shall know how to deal with them.'

More significantly, Honu told his audience that soon the Japanese would be launching a great offensive. 'We shall destroy the decadent British Army in front of us, capture Chittagong and march on Calcutta. Then we shall expel the tyrannical British from India also.'

This pronouncement made Holmes prick up his ears. It might be mere propaganda, but it seemed to tie-in with what Baba Khan had said about troop movements and the Japs' increased demands for rice throughout the peninsula. The Intelligence boys at 15th Corps must certainly be told; it might fit in with other information that they had. In the event, as we have already seen, what Honu said was a true declaration of intent.

After Honu had finished, the Japanese soldiers began distributing pamphlets. Shaffi secured a few of them and brought them afterwards to Holmes, but they were only lurid propaganda stuff. The crowd began to break up and it was time for Holmes and his party to make their way back.

Holmes was glowing with a sense of elation. To the satisfaction of a dangerous job well done was added the tingle of a dramatic situation. The cloud of fatigue that had hovered over him earlier was swept away. He had collected a great treasure of valuable information. He had experienced the thrill of penetrating deep into the enemy's territory. He had seen, smelt and almost touched the enemy themselves. He had outwitted them in a dangerous game. He had proved that, with reasonable caution, he could pass unnoticed among them and their accomplices in full daylight.

None the less, he was fully conscious how much he owed to the staunch loyalty and resourcefulness of Muhammad Shaffi. He felt a warm glow of gratitude to the gallant young jemadar. Without his resourceful initiative and his zealous care of his leader, Holmes thought that he could never have carried out such a mission. Shaffi seemed utterly regardless of himself. And with him Holmes bracketed all those humble villagers who, at great peril to themselves, readily offered their aid, and indeed

c

all that they had, to the service of those men from a distant land who had protected them from oppression in the past and to whom they now looked for liberation from the Japanese. He prayed that, when all was done, the politicians of the world, and of Whitehall in particular, would not let down these good and faithful people of simple origin.

5

First into Maungdaw

On his return to Dewdrop Inn Holmes found an unexpected visitor being hospitably entertained by Khyber Khan. This was a RAF pilot officer named Brown who had crash-landed on the beach near by and had been rescued by 'Burke' and 'Hare'. Half his tail had been shot away when his squadron had attacked a Japanese force which had carried out a bombing raid on Chittagong.

There was now a good deal of ominous air activity on both sides. From his vantage point at Teknaf Holmes and his friends watched with delight as the RAF Vengeance dive-bombers swooped down on enemy positions across the river, throwing up vast spouts of smoke and dust and débris, though the results proved to be disappointing. A trifle farther to the north and five miles directly to the east of Dewdrop Inn other evidences of battle grew nearer. The sounds of gunfire and shell-burst could be plainly heard, accompanied at night by the glitter of gun-flashes that momentarily illuminated the distant hills and were sharply reflected in the mirror of the sea.

After the bombing, news began to come through to Holmes from his scouts in the Maungdaw area that the Japanese were beginning to thin out in the town after the bombing and that nearly all the civilians had fled. Talking to Colonel Frink, CO of the 25th Dragoons, who had just replaced the West Yorkshires as the Teknaf garrison, he observed that, although Maungdaw, at that moment being bombed, was tremendously important to the British as a port, it had no such value to the Japs, who had no shipping to speak of, and it was useful to them only as a storehouse and a town with some good buildings.

'No longer good,' he added with a smile.

'But you'd suppose,' said Frink, 'that they would at least deny it to us.'

'Oh, they've got their defences of course, sir. We know something about them, but not all that we should like. Jolly dangerous place for our people.'

Fifth Division was at this moment girding itself for the march on Maungdaw. By New Year's Day, 1944 (while Holmes was in Lambaguna), having driven in the enemy outposts, they had closed up to the redoubt near Hathipauk, which barred the approach to the great prize. The redoubt consisted of a number of hillocks with skilfully designed supporting fire and it took Briggs's troops six days and nights of very hard fighting against a tough and resourceful enemy before they at last fixed a stranglehold around it. They were about to close in for the kill when unseasonable rain and a high wind enabled the garrison to slip away. The way to Maungdaw, three and a half miles away, was open. The West Yorkshires were ordered to capture it.

While these operations were in hand at the birth of the year, Holmes received an urgent summons on the night of the 5th to meet Donald at divisional headquarters. It was already dark and the fireflies were dancing madly, but Holmes set out at once in a sampan under a bright moon. Having made a slow trip against the tide through tortuous water channels, he met Donald at midnight in a camouflaged tent with the flying insects crowding round the hurricane lamps.

Donald began by complimenting him warmly on his recent expedition. 'Bloody good, Watson,' he said. 'The real McCoy.' He then went on to say that there were two matters that he wanted to discuss. First, he told Holmes that the West Yorkshires were to make the attack on Maungdaw and Holmes was to provide a number of sampans to ferry the battalion's stores over two chaungs that they would have to cross.

'That's easy enough,' he said. 'But the other affair is a damned sight more tricky.'

The big man paused a moment, a moment that seemed to Holmes to be charged with meaning, and then went on:

'What d'you make of the situation in Maungdaw?'

'Difficult to say, sir. It's pretty clear that all the civvies cleared out when the bombing began and it looks as though the Japs have removed what's left of their stores and probably their admin troops.'

'We've got to know much more than that if we can. Unless Moonshi Cree's chaps are accurately informed they may catch a packet. What are the chances of getting a really detailed low-down on the place?'

Holmes considered a moment and remarked:

'We've got a good man just outside, sir, in Karipara, but I don't know how exact his knowledge would be. Forget his name.'

'I know the chap; he'd cut his mother's throat for five rupees.'

An awkward silence. Then Holmes, thinking quickly, said:

'I think I'd better go myself, sir.'

'Good God! That would be a bloody fool thing to do.'

'All the same, I feel it's up to me, sir.'

'It's one hell of a risk, my dear chap; you'd never get away with it.'

'I got away with it at Lambaguna, sir, and I feel I owe it to the West Yorks. Besides, it will be a chance to show what V Force can do.'

'Well, it's up to you to decide, Watson. I won't order you not to do it, but I'd damned well think twice about it if I were you. But if you are such a BF as to go in, for Christ's sake don't get caught. Call it off at once if you look like running into trouble.'

Holmes returned to Dewdrop Inn full of thought. Had he been rash in offering to get right into an enemy-defended locality? Not just 'behind the lines'. Was it possible actually to penetrate the town? The Lambaguna expedition had given him some confidence in his chances of passing unnoticed; but was he being too cocky? He now felt a little daunted at the prospect, but he would have to go through with it.

The job had to be done quickly, but he must go about it damned carefully. Not *too* carefully, however. Boldness might be his best friend. Make straight for the place, as a fisherman would. Calculate the time and the tides. Take the jemadar with him, of course. Anyone else? The fewer the better, but he had found the presence of Corporal Disbury of great value when he went to meet Baba Khan. Better repeat the same pattern.

Accordingly he asked Frink for a good, reliable man to keep him company. Frink produced Corporal Shirvill, a very tall soldier with the presence of a guardsman, very erect and moving always as if on parade. Holmes took to him at once and thought him utterly reassuring, though it was obvious that no kind of disguise would ever look right on him. He told Shirvill what was expected of him and the corporal agreed at once. 'Just suit me, sir,' he said.

Holmes always acted quickly on these occasions. As a preliminary step, he sent one of his most trusted couriers to an agent who lived in a village at the southern tip of Maungdaw, with instructions to meet him there. Then, fortified by an excellent dinner of fried fish and roast chicken, with a glass or two of Indian rum, the three men, all in native dress, optimistic-ally set out from Teknaf in a kisti on the night of 7 January. The huge moon was almost at the full, flooding the whole river with a light nearly as brilliant as that of day. Holmes would have preferred darkness; he would have to exercise more caution. Shirvill's enormous frame proved to be very awkward in the primitive dug-out canoe and he nearly upset it as he embarked. The night was cold and damp and they put on their army pullovers. Shaffi took up his customary post in the prow.

As they approached the Mayu shore the gun-flashes became nearer, larger, more brilliant and the sounds of gun-shot and shell-burst louder, more emphatic, more full of meaning. The rocky hills flung back their angry voices in rolling echoes all along the range. This was going to be a very different affair from the expedition to Lambaguna. There they had been several miles behind the fighting lines. This time they were to be right in it, and on the enemy side. The thought gave Holmes uneasy stirrings, disturbing the romantic Scarlet Pimpernel feeling of the earlier evening. Why the hell, he asked himself, did I undertake this damn-fool mission?

Rather by instinct, he shaped course to bring the kisti directly to the makeshift 'docks' of Maungdaw, which lay not on the river Naf itself but on the southern bank of a chaung, known as the Tat, which flowed into the main river.

He was sanguine enough to think that he might be able to land openly on the wharf. A bridge spanned the Tat and

Holmes knew that here the Japanese maintained a standing patrol; but he knew also that the bridge had recently been badly damaged, perhaps destroyed, and there was a good chance that the patrol might have been withdrawn. Would he be able to slip past unobserved? Or perhaps be allowed to pass as a fisherman?

Crossing the brightly silvered water, Holmes saw the Mayu coast, low and irregular, as a thin streak of oyster-grey, broken by bold masses of charcoal where the big mangoes stood. Slowly the kisti closed the shore, then swung to port and, keeping to the northern bank, entered the chaung. Now was the time for the utmost caution. Crouching low, all on the *qui vive*, the little party crept in, very slowly and in total silence. Maungdaw lay on their starboard hand, dark, secret, eerie, peopled with enemies. North Island, flat and dreary, lay to port. No longer was Holmes sanguine. This, he thought ruefully, is hellish dangerous. He found himself involuntarily shivering a little.

It was very cold now, with a wind whipping in from the sea. Wisps of spray from the small waves saturated their clothing. Gun-flashes punctuated the moonlight and were brazenly reflected on the muddy surface of the chaung. As the kisti crept in along the bank of North Island, however, it was one of these flashes that, illuminating the dark moon shadows, warned him of imminent danger; for, where the bridge had stood, a single plank now spanned the chaung and beside the plank, a long rifle slung across his shoulder, stood a Japanese sentry.

Holmes instantly ordered: 'Backwater.'

As the paddles reversed there was a gurgle of water, sounding to their sensitive ears like the thunder of a waterfall. Stroke by stroke they went astern until it was safe to make about. In a few minutes they were out into the Naf again and paused for a moment. Holmes turned to Shirvill, who was behind him and asked, 'You all right, corporal?'

'Got the wind up for a moment, sir, and had the tommy-gun ready for the little bastard.'

'Good show, but thank goodness you didn't use it.'

He held a short colloquy with Shaffi. As a result, they headed

farther south, aiming to come into Maungdaw from the
landward side, by way of the big Magyi chaung, a mile south of
the town, where they had first tried to land on their visit to
Baba Khan.

Half an hour's paddling brought them to the mouth of the
'Big Woman', 400 yards wide, and again they turned to port,
making this time for the north bank.

They began to edge in. The massive forms of banyans and
mangoes stood out black against the bright sky, their dense
shadows mottling the moonlit scene. The shore resolved itself
into a thick line of charcoal. Holmes felt his heart thumping.
Landing was always a step into the unknown. Would there be
an enemy reception committee waiting for them?

Guided by Shaffi, they made for a spot where a thicket of
mangroves was crowded into a bend of the chaung. Everything
here was very quiet. The only sounds were those of the distant
gunfire and the drumming of their own heartbeats.

They waited a few minutes among the muddy mangroves,
listening. Then Shaffi slipped ashore to reconnoitre. He returned
after a minute and beckoned to the others to come on. Holmes
waded ashore, but Shirvill, unaccustomed to the canoe,
disembarked clumsily, with a loud splash of mud. As he did so
a cormorant rose noisily, uttering its harsh cry. Holmes at once
crouched and the others followed suit. Still no sign of human
activity. Holmes stood up after a long pause and glanced round
hastily. 'On we go,' he whispered.

The ground was still damp from the recent rain and in their
bare feet they made no sound as they moved cautiously inland,
but Holmes felt uneasy at the deadly quiet that lay over the
land. What has happened, he asked himself. The silence was
unearthly. For him, silence always spelt danger. It signified the
unknown. Known perils might be avoided; those unknown
might catch one unawares at any moment. Were the Japanese
snoozing away in the bunkers with no one on watch? Or were
they lying in ambush for him? How trustworthy was the agent?
Anything might lie concealed in the black slabs of the tree
shadows and Holmes felt nervous whenever they plunged into
their obscurity. Suddenly Shaffi, who was leading, stumbled
and fell to the ground. Holmes ran forward to help him, but

Shaffi was erect again in a moment, laughing quietly to himself. He whispered to Holmes:

'Bomb hole, sahib, from British Vengeance plane.'

They walked on in the brilliant moonlight and very soon began to encounter a few bashas. Their high bamboo fences declared them to be the houses of Muslims, which Holmes found reassuring. All were closed and dark. This was the village of Karipara, the southern suburb of Maungdaw. They slowed down here, for this was the rendezvous with their agent. A faint light glimmered in one of the bashas. Shaffi entered the compound, mounted the steps to the house and presently came out with the agent. After whispered greetings and cordial handshakes the agent said to Holmes:

'Sahib, many *Japani* have been killed by the British bombs and I think that the rest have all gone away.'

'Gone away! Are you sure? Tell me what you actually saw.'

'I saw lots of men collect together from different directions and march out to the east. But there may be some more left.'

'How many marched out, do you think?'

'Perhaps a hundred and fifty, perhaps more, sahib. I could not see very well; it was only an hour ago.'

'There would have been more than that. Let us go and see. Take me right into Maungdaw.'

This was a patrol operation and Holmes now led, with the guide at his side and Shirvill protectively in the rear. The two soldiers cocked their tommy-guns and Shaffi had his revolver in hand. The four moved forward guardedly into the weirdly chequered moonlight, its brilliant clarity broken by solid black shadows, and as they advanced they grew more and more astonished at the deadly spectacle that increasingly disclosed itself in the ghostly moonscape.

Riven and torn by the RAF, deserted by the civil population and uncared for by the Japanese during their seven months of occupation, Maungdaw was a place of rotting desolation. The walls and corrugated iron roofs of buildings, if they had not been totally destroyed by bombing, leaned at grotesque angles against the night sky, casting even more grotesque shadows. Small trees had been uprooted, and the branches of larger ones lay athwart the chaotic scene.

The two main streets festered with a rank growth of weeds. Tall grasses enveloped the verandas of what had been European-type bungalows. Loofah plants grew everywhere. Japanese equipment lay about as thickly as the litter of a racecourse. Bundles of straw bedding had been burst open and were scattered among the wreckage. Here and there Japanese graves were to be seen, each mound of earth topped with a sun helmet. Tangles of barbed wire festooned the deserted defences and a green slime coated the planks and piers of the ramshackle docks. Everywhere the moon played strange tricks, making many objects look like hostile figures.

Even more outrageous to the perceptions was the pungent stink that impregnated the air of the whole place, like the stink that assailed the nostrils when the Japanese burnt their dead, and mingled with it were the odours of putrefying refuse and excreta. There was absolutely no movement of any sort except the scurrying of marauding rats, which startled the party from time to time.

A place of the dead, thought Holmes, with the smell of the dead.

Incautiously, forgetting his training for a moment, he stepped down on to one of the deserted defences to investigate and felt something catch his naked toe. There was a violent explosion and all four were thrown to the ground.

In a low voice Holmes ordered:

'Lie still.'

The detonation, he thought, would certainly rouse any form of life that might have been lying hidden or asleep, but, as the dust settled, so did the silence. He got up and said:

'Booby trap. Bet the whole place is lousy with them. Keep away from anything that looks like a trench or a bunker.'

With due care they made a systematic search of the town, visiting all the known defences and the docks. Over the Tat Chaung they discerned the single plank still in place where the bridge had stood and where the sentry had rattled them only three hours ago.

The party had by now abated their caution to some extent, though Holmes well knew the enemy's practice of leaving snipers behind. He said to the others:

'Well, it's obvious that there are no Japs left in Maungdaw. But where have they gone? We have got to find that out, too. The only way left now is eastwards.'

The guide said: 'They started that way, sahib, on the road to Razabil. But they may have turned north-east or south-east.'

'All right, let's go and find out. Show us the way.'

They started out and had not gone a mile to the east when, from a thicket of kanyin trees near the village of Kanyindan, strange voices were heard. They approached cautiously, crouching, and Shaffi crept to the front. After a few yards his nostrils recognized at once that tell-tale, sickly-sweet odour of the Japanese soldier. He shook his head from side to side and motioned the others to get back.

As the little party walked quickly back Holmes was thinking hard. The night was now far spent and he had all the information that he could expect to get; more than he had hoped for. The enemy, for some reason, had vacated Maungdaw but were only a mile to the east. What their strength was and how long they intended to stay in Kanyindan he could not tell, but the booby traps were strong evidence that they did not propose to return to Maungdaw for the time being.

With these reflexions in mind he said to his companions:

'There's no point in staying here any longer. We have got some jolly valuable information and what we must do now is to get it to our troops as soon as possible.'

He explained to Shirvill that the West Yorkshires were due to attack Maungdaw the very next night. He knew that they were in the locality of 'Elephant Gap', which was four miles to the north by road, but he expected that they would now be feeling their way south and having a fairly sticky time, having to cross two or three awkward, mud-banked chaungs by the sampans which he had arranged for and which they would have to carry laboriously from chaung to chaung.

Shaffi said: 'We go back to the kisti, then, sahib?'

'No; that would take far too long. We don't go back; we go forward. We walk out to the north until we meet our own army.'

'Shall we not meet the *Japani* first, sahib?'

'We've got to risk that. I think that the battle at Hathipauk is over, but there are sure to be Japanese troops trying to stop ours from advancing any further. We shall just have to chance our arm and try to avoid them.' Turning to Shirvill, he added: 'You happy about that, corporal?'

'Anything you say, sir.'

Shaffi's smile gleamed in the night and he said: 'I will smell them out for you, sahib.'

Shirvill said: 'Funny if we got shot up by our own chaps, sir.'

'We shall just have to use our loafs, corporal,' Holmes answered. 'Afraid I don't know the password.'

The decision made, Holmes dismissed the guide with cordial thanks for his valuable help, instructing him to find the kisti and tell the boatman to return to Teknaf. The three others then re-entered Maungdaw, feeling in high spirits, but, passing the old civil hospital, Holmes's bare foot trod on an upturned nail. The small wound caused him a great deal of pain and served sharply to bring home to him the fact that, although now filled with a buoyant sense of exhilaration, they were all pretty tired, physically and emotionally. They still had a long walk ahead of them, with the likelihood of meeting Japanese troops on the way.

He therefore asked Shaffi if he knew of any place where they could rest and get a little refreshment and was relieved when the jemadar told him that he had a friend in Letha, the first village north of Maungdaw. Here lived a faithful old pensioner of the British Government named Mashraf Ali, a former Excise messenger, and his brother, who was known to the British as 'Father Christmas' because of his venerable beard.

Holmes and Shirvill laughed quietly. 'Sounds like home, sir,' said the tall corporal.

So, with the feeling of a valuable mission accomplished, the three left the derelict town by the track that led out north-east from it, Holmes limping confidently behind the jemadar. Twenty minutes walking in the eerie emptiness under a declining moon brought them to Letha, all shuttered and silent and dark. Here Shaffi entered an obviously Muslim compound, mounted the steps to the basha within and cautiously knocked. Mashraf Ali and his bearded brother welcomed them all in whispers and with tears of joy that touched Holmes deeply. They could scarcely believe that at long last the British Army was coming back. They had lived in terror during the Japanese occupation and were ready to offer their lives for King George. 'You must march on Akyab straight away,' they said. The old men were greatly impressed by the stature and bearing of Corporal Shirvill, and he, for his part, took them to his heart at once. He shook them warmly by the hand and said in English: 'Don't worry, Johnnie, we'll soon be back.'[1]

Thus they quietly conversed in that remote little basha while the good old men brewed them some tea and served sweet coconut rice from their small store and one of them washed Holmes's injured foot and bound it with a clean, white cloth. From outside the honeyed scent of the sweet jasmine, 'Queen of the Night', drifted in and for a little while the severity of war seemed far away.

Much refreshed, Holmes and his companions bade the villagers as cordial a farewell as they could in low tones and continued their walk. The moon had now gone. The night was cold and miserable with a clammy, breast-high mist enveloping the ground and imposing extra caution on their movements. A heavy quiet lay over all the countryside. No guns spoke. They passed along shrouded paddy-fields, skirted dim groves of banana trees and coconut palms and, tommy-guns and pistol held high, perilously forded a chaung that chilled them to the marrow.

Notwithstanding his injured foot, Holmes felt like a disembodied spirit as, in utter silence, his head and shoulders glided above the cloud-like mist and the sparkling canopy of stars seemed to press down around him. He sensed again the dangers of silence, accentuated by the veil of mist. Therefore he felt grateful for the keen perceptions of Shaffi ahead of him and for the stalwart presence of Corporal Shirvill behind. It seemed to him miraculous that they met no enemy, but the mist that might hide the enemy would have hidden them too.

They ran into British troops sooner than expected. Cree's forward elements, after stumbling and cursing as they carried their heavy sampans from chaung to chaung and slithered down the muddy banks, were less than two miles from Maungdaw. In

[1] British soldiers called all the brown peoples by the friendly name of 'Johnnie'.

the early hours of 8 January, an imperious challenge rang out in the dark. Holmes walked forward and found himself at the entrenchments of a platoon of the West Yorkshires. He disclosed his identity, but, rightly suspicious of the bedraggled figures in lungyis, the soldiers, themselves wet and tired, kept them covered with their weapons while they sent for an officer. Fortunately the subaltern who came forward had met Holmes at Teknaf and provided him with a guide to Gerald Cree's tactical headquarters, which was nearly three miles back at a chaungside village near Hathipauk called Kayugyaung.

There, having limped forward, fatigued, cold, an incongruous figure in soiled native dress, muddy feet, with a blackened face and suspiciously carrying a tommy-gun, he was accosted by Lieutenant John Wiberg, Gerald Cree's signals officer, who instinctively drew his revolver and was about to shoot, when Holmes said sharply: 'Put it up man! I'm Major Holmes of V Force and I've some important information for Colonel Cree.'

Wiberg took him into a dimly lit tent, where he found a tired-looking Cree, who, having returned from visiting his forward company, was in conversation with Brigadier Marindin, the head of V Force, and Rockbound Donald, who was sitting on Cree's bed. It was 5 a.m.

Holmes addressed himself to Cree, saying, in effect, though certainly not in so many words:

'Well sir, you can call off your artillery barrage and march into Maungdaw with colours flying and drums beating.'

The next night C Company of the West Yorkshires, under Major J. P. Roche, formally occupied Maungdaw, though before reaching the town they had to brush off some light opposition from a party of enemy whom Holmes had fortunately avoided; and at Kanyindan, B Company duly ran into machine-gun fire from the Japanese post that Shaffi had smelt out in the kanyin wood.

Soon afterwards cameramen and news hounds from many kennels arrived to record the great feat of the soldiers who had recaptured the prize of Maungdaw. But of V Force not a word was heard, not a picture taken. Only a few front-line soldiers knew.

6

The Black Tarantulas

The Misfire – Dewdrop Inn Moves Up
The Colourful Brotherhood – First Blood
Alethangyaw Overrun

The capture of Maungdaw marks the beginning of a completely
new canto in the many-patterned ballad of the West Mayu V
Force. They still carried out their primary part as intelligence
agents, but they were now more able to give vent to the offensive
spirit which was lurking in such men as Denis Holmes, Muhammad Shaffi, young Habibullah and many more. They became
combatants. They formed partnerships with fighting troops and
led them into fierce little battles well behind the enemy lines.
They sallied out to kill and to capture the enemy. They suffered
their own casualties. They went to the rescue of RAF pilots in
distress. They haunted the enemy coast and probed into the
interior with tommy-gun and hand grenade in stealthy raids by
night.

They made their first little raid almost immediately after the
capture of Maungdaw. It was a failure, but valuable lessons
were learnt from it. The circumstances that led up to it were
due to the change in the tactical situation after Maungdaw.

As we have seen, the Japanese 112th Brigade, under Colonel
Tanahashi, was deployed along the Mayu coast as a flank
guard. Some of its positions were small infantry posts but others
were supplemented by field guns sited to engage ships at sea or
to repel landings. The capture of Maungdaw led to considerable
increase in the numbers of British small craft using the River
Naf and gave more substance to the notion of a possible British
landing in force.

At this stage of the operations it became the policy of Christison at 15th Corps and of Briggs in 5th Division to play upon whatever apprehensions the Japanese might have and to oblige them to keep 'looking over their shoulders'. Both 5th and 7th Divisions were now squaring up to assault the two main buttresses of the Golden Fortress, that on Briggs's front being the formidable stronghold on the hilly ground at Razabil (two miles eastward of Maungdaw), where the Japanese had scooped out a rabbit warren of underground gun emplacements, bunkers, tunnels and deep shelters. Briggs was therefore anxious that Tanahashi's brigade should be deterred from reinforcing the Razabil defences and other Japanese positions in the difficult foothills south-east of Maungdaw and that they should be kept constantly on the jump on their coastal flank.

This meant launching raids by the 'commando' method. They began in a very small way but soon gathered force and impetus. Unlike many other raids made during the war, they had an operational purpose directly related to the tactical plans. V Force, being the only source of information on the enemy's coastal dispositions, became the key factor in these raids, the accuracy of their information proving almost uncanny. Holmes was 'put in the picture' immediately after the occupation of Maungdaw by Freddy Noble, Briggs's chief staff officer, and he saw Briggs himself the very day after and twice again in the next few days. On the first occasion, having complimented him on his reconnaissance of Maungdaw and Lambaguna, Briggs promised him the full support of his staff and asked him if there was anything that he wanted.

It happened that Holmes had just received word from young Habibullah, his chief scout at No-Can-Do, that the Japanese had established a small post at the near-by mainland village of Dodan, eleven miles within the enemy lines. He therefore asked the general whether there was any chance of carrying out a small raid to secure an identification. Briggs readily agreed and said that he could have a section from the West Yorkshires.

Filled with the sense of confidence that Briggs had the faculty of imparting, Holmes hurried off gleefully to Gerald Cree, who gave him Lieutenant French and six men. Together they sallied out from Maungdaw in two kistis at midnight that very same night (10/11 January) on a falling tide and under a brilliant moon. The interpreter, Muhammad Yusuf, accompanied them. Two hours paddling in the cold, damp weather brought them to No-Can-Do.

The Misfire

Dodan, noted for its melons, brings to our immediate attention a larger and much more important coastal village some three miles away, in the locality of which were to take place the brisk and bustling forays that affrighted the nights for the next three months. This village was called Alethangyaw, meaning approximately 'The Middle Crossing', but inevitably was anglicized in various forms, the most apt of which was 'I'll-thank-you'. So important is it to our narrative that we must pause to have a fairly close look at it right from the start.

Some thirteen miles south of Maungdaw, Alethangyaw was a long, straggling, sun-baked village of local importance, lying about a mile inland at the point where the River Naf gives way to the open sea and where the muddy mangrove swamps are replaced by gleaming white sands on steeply shelving beaches, against which the waves of the Bay of Bengal break in high surf. It lay athwart a neck of land between two large chaungs significant to our narrative – the Alethangyaw and the Taungbo Chaungs – and it straddled the tolerably good track, motorable in dry weather, that trickled down from Maungdaw and was euphemistically called 'the coast road'. Perhaps it was this situation that justified the name of 'Middle Crossing', as far as we can translate it.

From the sea Alethangyaw had an attractive appearance, enfolded with thickets of bamboo, groves of palm and banana and many fine trees, so that it seemed to be overlaid with a green haze, specially when, in autumn, the surrounding rice-fields were in their full grassy leaf. Among its bashas were a few superior houses of timber, a school and a small police station. At its eastern end was a government bungalow, at its western a post office and in the centre a pagoda. Most of the houses had good air-raid shelters built beneath them or in their compounds.

Most of the Mughs had deserted the village and so had some

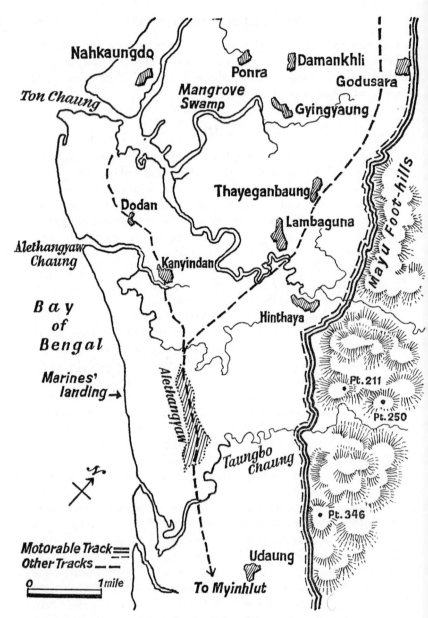

Fig. 4. The Main Raiding Ground. Outlines at low tide. Nahkaungdo ('No-Can-Do') and other places become islands at high water.

of the Muslims. Among those remaining, living in a good timber house, was little 'Rob Roy', one of V Force's most celebrated informers, whom we already noticed earlier and who was on close terms with Denis Holmes. On several occasions in later days he also freely contacted British soldiers directly, though he knew that he was being watched.

A maze of chaungs, like searching tentacles, meandered among the mud-flats that lay to the west and north of Alethangyaw, creating islands when the tide was high, but many little hamlets were scattered in the neighbourhood. Alethangyaw was also the heart of a surprisingly large complex of small Japanese coast-watching detachments, such as those at Dodan, Ponra and another Kanyindan, to which the grenades and bayonets of the raiding forces were drawn as by a magnet on account of their proximity to the obscure little island of No-Can-Do, which Holmes had discovered and noted as an ideal springboard for a dive into the interior.

French's little party, accompanied by Holmes and Yusuf, crossed to the mainland from No-Can-Do in kistis soon after 2 a.m. on the 11th, their number added to by Habibullah and another local scout named Ahmed Hussein. The moon was still in its full splendour as they disembarked and moved silently across the open melon-fields. When within a hundred yards of the enemy position the fighting party halted under cover of some trees, while two of the three Chittagonians went forward to reconnoitre. Unfortunately, not having Shaffi's skill in these matters, they ran into a Jiff look-out, who sounded a furious alarm with a whistle. The Japanese rushed from their warm, straw-covered trench and manned their posts. For some two hours there was utter silence, during which the moon hid her lamp, the cold night mist gathered and Holmes looked anxiously for the return of his scouts. Soon after 5 a.m. French whispered that he thought that they ought to withdraw, as it would soon be dawn. Holmes reluctantly agreed and French took his six men back to the boats, with Habibullah as guide, and re-embarked in one of them. Holmes, however, declined to go. He could not leave his scouts in the lurch and said that he would wait behind for another hour.

It was the first time that he had been quite alone in hostile country. He waited in a dark and eerie silence, chilled to the bone by the night mist but ears and eyes on the alert. The hour passed, and more than the hour. Regretfully he decided that he must wait no longer. He was in uniform and carrying a tommy-gun and two grenades. He made his way back to the remaining kisti, reaching it at 6.30, when it was almost daylight, and had just stepped into it when a patrol of three Japanese appeared on the bank just above him. For a moment both parties stared at each other in amazement. Holmes's drowsy boatman then sprung into life, pushed off from the bank and, with a few strokes, whisked the canoe into midstream.

The Japanese gesticulated and ran forward. One of the three raised his rifle to his shoulder, but put it down again. Holmes thought that he was going to get away with it and told the boat-man to act naturally and not to hurry. A moment later, however, when the range was still scarcely fifty yards, the other two Japs opened fire and the first man followed suit. At each red flash from the rifles a little jet of water splashed up a few yards from the canoe.

'Heads down! Fast as you can,' ordered Holmes, obeying his own command.

It was a ticklish moment. Holmes experienced that tingling sensation in the back when one is shot at from behind. The bullets continued to splash around, but fortunately the Japs maintained their notoriety for being very bad shots and in another half-minute the kisti was swallowed up in the morning mist.

Holmes, having reported to 5th Division, returned to Dewdrop Inn full of thought. Next time there must be better planning, more careful reconnaissance. He must be sure to take Jemadar Shaffi with him. He must not approach from the front, but from the rear, the Japanese being particularly vulnerable when hit by the unexpected. He was much concerned for the fate of his two scouts but a few days later learned with great satisfaction that they had escaped from the Japanese during a bombing raid. He was sorry to hear soon afterwards, however, that French had been killed in the stiff fighting in difficult country in which the West Yorkshires were engaged south-east of Maungdaw.

Dewdrop Inn Moves Up

Teknaf was much too far away for keeping close touch with operations, as V Force was now required to do. With Donald's approval, Holmes therefore moved Dewdrop Inn across the river to North Island, not far from the ruined bridge that had crossed the Tat Chaung to connect the island with Maungdaw. 'Father Christmas', meeting him again, said: 'Sahib, you must come and live near me.' Holmes sent Khyber Khan to the old man, who found him two substantial bashas within typical Muslim compounds and a third less pretentious one as a kitchen, where 'Danny' was reinstalled as cook. Khyber, chivvying the scouts, soon had everything ship-shape.

North Island was very low-lying and dead flat, but a good scattering of trees relieved the austerity. Here, while the West Yorkshires carried the tide of battle noisily to east and south of him amid clouds of dirty, yellow dust, Holmes felt himself to be very close to things, ideally situated for excursions down the enemy coast and well in the stream of communications with 5th Division. Captain Antony Brett-James, one of the divisional signals officers, ran a telephone line to him and supped with 'the quiet major', who that very evening was preparing to leave on 'one of his hazardous missions, concerning which he speaks few words'.[1]

Here, against the background of gunfire and bombs, Holmes made the acquaintance of some scouts whom he had not met before. Prominent among them was 'Harpo Marx'. He owed his name to his long, shaggy hair (on top of which he wore a funny, conical hat) and to the big grin that always enlivened his face. He was a brave fellow, acting as go-between with the agents and informers for some twelve miles along the coast. Harpo had an almost constant companion in a youngster called 'Tommy-gun'. The pair went about everywhere together, unless Holmes sent them off on separate jobs. Another whom he welcomed was Osiullah, a bright and fearless young fisherman from Alethangyaw.

V Force, its value proved and appreciated and expected to

[1] Antony Brett-James: *Report My Signals*.

widen its scope, was being expanded and strengthened. Its reinforcements included two extra officers, both from Punjabi regiments. One of these was Captain John Comer, 14th Punjabis, whom Holmes made his liaison officer with 5th Division, and the other was the colourful Lieutenant 'Martin' Luthera, of his own 1st Punjabis, a young Sikh who was a considerable linguist and well equipped as an Intelligence officer. Contrary to Sikh tradition, he wore his hair short and had no beard. Holmes sent him at first to Teknaf for the examining of suspects and similar duties, but both he and Comer later had their share of fighting and Luthera won the Military Cross. Several other spirited young officers, including Jack Lawson, of the West Yorkshires, had applied for transfer, but had been refused either by their COs or by Holmes.

V Force became plunged into a whirl of diverse activities. They salvaged crashed RAF machines and rescued one Indian pilot. On the Teknaf peninsula 'Burke' and 'Hare' salvaged a Japanese aircraft. A Polish RAF officer named Kukulka asked for 100 men to salvage an aircraft crashed in a chaung, and got them in two hours. The sappers wanted labour for Major John Orgill to rebuild the Tat Chaung bridge and got them as quickly. Flotillas of sampans were called for at short notice for the use of troops in ferrying stores across the numerous chaungs.

A heavy demand soon built up from the fighting units for V Force men to act as guides and informants on local conditions. Before long many units became reluctant to make any move forward without a scout at their head. As far as he could, Holmes gave each of these units a man whom they could call their own. Thus he sent 'Johnny' on more or less permanent attachment to the West Yorkshires, with 'Tommy-gun' as an occasional extra. The forbidding mulvi Siddiq went to the West Africans (of whom more very soon) and Osiullah to the Burma Intelligence Corps, who were doing very good work in their own field.

At the same time the far more important work of sifting and analysing the information brought in by scouts and the screening of suspect characters increased prodigiously. There were frequent arrests. Information was flooding in to V Force from near and far. As soon as the Japanese showed their noses anywhere the news was swiftly brought to Holmes. It was inspiring to feel that his watch on enemy movements was now closely related to immediate operations and that V Force had virtually become part of the division, working in close relations both with its headquarters and with its forward battalions

A high and confident spirit animated all troops and there was a widespread eagerness to keep going fast. Maungdaw was being rapidly cleaned up under its enterprising commandant, Lt-Colonel R. E. Jardine. Immediately to the east and south the fighting waxed fierce as the battle reached vital ground. Convoys of wounded jolted painfully through the town for evacuation by sea. Holmes and his scouts, on the fringe of the battle, listened daily to the continuous trumpeting of the guns and watched the Mitchell, Liberator and Vengeance bombers attack the honeycomb defences of Razabil and the adjacent foothills. On the 15th, to their huge glee, sixteen enemy fighter aircraft were shot down as they tried to attack the bombers. Huge clouds of dust, stirred up by the jolting vehicles, the trampling of the mules, the blasts of guns and the bursts of shells, smothered all things and cast a veil over the sun itself, becoming a sore affliction to all.

Holmes's friends of the West Yorkshires were locked in bitter fighting in the villages and foothills to the south-east of Maungdaw, a mile or two beyond the Magyi Chaung, using quantities of sampans provided by V Force. Briggs, visiting Cree immediately after the fall of Maungdaw, had expected much of them and they had become over-extended, taking sharp casualties but always succeeding in carrying their point against repeated enemy attempts to cut them up. The 3rd/9th Jats were backing them up and holding the important iron bridge that spanned the Magyi Chaung, while Holmes's old battalion, the 2nd/1st Punjabis, scrambled precariously along the crest of the Mayu hills.

In the middle of these noisy activities Holmes learnt to his amusement some very personal news from the Japanese Intelligence. His name and those of his scouts closest to him were now well known throughout the villages of West Mayu. The bush telegraph hummed with their doings (and with false news deliberately planted by Siddiq and others). Wherever Holmes went on his darkling trips, there was no need of explanation when his name was mentioned. Hence he was not surprised when he learnt that the Japanese also knew all about him. What amused him was the news brought in by one of his scouts that the enemy Intelligence had set a price on his head, dead or alive. He chuckled and said to Jack Comer:

'Makes me feel hellish important – like Robin Hood and the Scarlet Pimpernel.'

'All the same, Denis,' Comer replied, 'don't go sticking your neck out.'

Smiling at the implication, Holmes answered:

'Your point is taken, Jack. I don't intend to oblige him.'

Shaffi also became notorious among the villagers. Though he had friends everywhere, people who feared to become embroiled in the dangerous game developed a reserve towards him. Others grew jealous of his remarkable success. He was so anxious about his brother's family at Dodan that Donald had them all secretly evacuated to the safety of Bawli Bazar.

The Colourful Brotherhood

After ten exacting days of these multifarious duties, the spectacular series of raids began in earnest, the one crowding fast upon the other. They were planned and executed by a spontaneous partnership of three dissociated elements that soon grew into an eager brotherhood. These elements consisted of V Force, a fighting force from the troops of 5th Division, and a 'naval' element provided on several occasions by the assorted craft of 290th Special Purposes Company, Inland Water Transport. Together they formed a private 'combined operations' task force which had no staff, but whose three commanders planned and executed their strikes swiftly and with maximum economy of force.

The water-borne unit of this partnership, like V Force, was typical of the makeshift expedients to which the army in Burma was so often obliged to resort. The 290th Company consisted of eight old, unwieldy, wood-fired civilian river steamers, four motor launches, and about a dozen Fleming lifeboats which were taken on tow and intended to be used as 'assault craft'. All were wholly innocent of navigational gear. They were manned by Bengali civilians, a very windy lot, and commanded by sporting young Indian Army officers whose ignorance of seamanship was total. Their CO, the debonair Major 'Binks' Firbank, found them 'nice chaps but a wildly undisciplined lot, who took a little bringing to heel'.

Binks himself, who had been seconded from Sam Browne's Cavalry, was a charming personality who had been a yachtsman since boyhood and his colourful and ebullient figure, clad usually in little else than very short shorts (held up by a rope) and a piratical scarf, became one of the familiar sights to all who trafficked in the muddy waters of the Naf. He and Holmes, who were kindred spirits in their love of independence and adventure, had become friends at Teknaf, where the company had been stationed and where one or more of its ships were usually to be seen at Jackson's Jetty.

The third member of this combined operations brotherhood was another unit, even more colourful, that Holmes had already met at Teknaf. This was the Reconnaissance Regiment of the 81st (West African) Division, wearing their fierce divisional badge of a black tarantula on a yellow ground, the cunning Gizzo of West African folklore. Equipped mainly with armoured cars and Bren-gun carriers (lightly armoured vehicles on tracks), they were unemployable in the Kaladan Valley, where the division, with no other transport than mules and their own strong head-porters, was committed to a hard slog under arduous conditions as left-flank guard for 15th Corps, so Christison had given them to Briggs to harry the Japanese on his sensitive southern flank. and keep the enemy's 112th Brigade locked up.

Few troops were better suited than the West Africans to that particular kind of game; warlike raiding was just what their fathers had been doing not long since. Holmes took to them at once. Except for some Northern Nigerians who were fair-skinned, they were ebony-black Negroes, huge, cheerful, laughing and simple-minded. They wore long shorts and pork-pie felt hats and were fully accustomed to going about barefooted and silently, and to carrying large loads on their crisply curled heads. They had enormous appetites. Food, which they called 'chop', was one of their two great joys in life, especially their

traditional ground-nut stew. A big mound of 'chop' before an
expedition put them in good form. They attacked their food
eagerly, thrusting great handfuls into their mouths. In close
action they often used the long-bladed machete, provided by a
benevolent government for chopping wood but, like the
Burmese *dah*, equally good for chopping off heads. They had a
great sense of humour and spoke a pidgin-English with the most
amusing expressions. They called the Japanese 'the Japan'.

These husky Negroes came from three West African colonies,
each forming its own squadron. Their A Squadron were
Nigerians, B came from the Gold Coast (now Ghana) and C
(which was still back in India) from Sierra Leone. Their
discipline was first-class and they were led by exceptionally
good British officers and NCOs – 'as fit and cheerful a team' in
Holmes's words 'as one could wish to meet anywhere, breezy
and full of confidence'. Their exceptionally able CO, Richard
Cartwright, had been at Sandhurst with him and in the same
company, but they had not seen each other for some twelve
years, so that their meeting at Teknaf two months before had
been the renewal of an old comradeship.

Cartwright himself had been seconded from the Inniskilling
Dragoon Guards. What might be called a typical cavalryman
(at least in fiction), he was the son and grandson of generals,
good-looking, debonair, a delightful character, a keen polo-
player and ex-Harrow. He was always smartly turned out in the
style of an 'Eighth Army type', with scarf, desert boots and
fly-whisk. Withal he had a brilliant brain, was full of originality
and drive and was filled with what one of his officers described
as 'massive courage'. Altogether, he was an outstanding soldier
and his merit was shown by his appointment to command at an
early age and, indeed, he was soon to be promoted brigadier,
only to be cut off in his prime by an obscure tropical disease.

Cartwright's brother officers were a mixture from good
British regiments and civil servants or civilians from West
African colonies. A visiting wit remarked (though he was not
quite right) that they were 'the only white officers leading
black troops against a yellow enemy in a brown man's land'.

The second-in-command, Bernard Shattock, was a Territorial
from the Queen's Royal Regiment. The Nigerian squadron was

commanded by Major Arthur Mooring, an experienced District Officer of the Colonial Service, full of lore about the Nigerians, who proved a very brave and able soldier. He was known as 'Satan', a nickname he owed to his slightly Mephistophelian appearance, his long face being marked by black, slanting eyebrows and pointed ears. Satan became Holmes's particular friend.

Two others of Cartwright's officers came from Rhodesia, a country that has a happy facility for producing officers of good calibre. The senior was the Gold Coasters' squadron leader, Major Alan McBean, square-shouldered, clean-cut, already wearing the ribbon of the Military Cross. The other was Jack Farquharson, robust and jolly in a Falstaffian manner (but quite unlike that old jellyfish when the bullets began to fly); he succeeded to command of the squadron when McBean was injured later on.

Unlike the units of the Indian Army, the West African regiments had a strong element of British NCOs. Those in Cartwright's regiment were of high quality, all from good British regiments, and, by backing-up and guiding the African NCOs, many of whom were illiterate, they set an example as junior leaders and acted as catalysts in the diverse elements. British NCOs also took care of the heavy weapons, the signals and the vehicle maintenance.

The Tarantulas were stationed in the southern part of Maungdaw, where they formed part of the garrison. Their well-laid-out headquarters testified to Cartwright's standards of orderliness, with dug-in and camouflaged tents, vehicle parks and tracks regularly watered to keep down the pervading dust, a volley-ball ground and a smart guard.

For all this, the West African troops did not go down at all well with the local people. To Indians and those of Indian stock, as most of the V Force men were, a Negro, or anyone negroid, is a *hubshi*, which means an ugly, base-born slave, neglected of Allah. Holmes realized this animosity very quickly and strove to overcome it. 'After all,' he said one morning to Shaffi, Khyber and Siddiq, 'they are our friends. Also remember that many of the Nigerians come from the Hausa tribe, who are not only a warrior race, but are also Muslims, like yourselves.'

Gradually the scouts' attitude moderated and after one raid Shaffi said to Holmes: 'These *hubshi* are not bad chaps after all, sahib. They are very good at killing the yellow dogs. But, sahib, how they eat!'

The Tarantulas, for their part, had an immediate liking for the scouts. They thought them very brave and skilful. The exception was the sinister-looking, black-eyed Siddiq, whom Holmes lent on permanent attachment to the regiment. Most of the Africans feared him and called him the 'black-bearded bastard with the cunning eye', but the Muslim Nigerians respected and liked him.

Just two days before their first raid the Africans had suffered a reverse when, in their first action, they had lost several carriers to enemy guns when supporting an attack by the Jats just south of Maungdaw. Henceforth they fought as infantry. In addition to the routine work of patrolling on 5th Division's southern flank, Cartwright and his men were eager for raiding action, but needed local guides, interpreters, boatmen and an intelligence service. All these V Force provided, and so began a closely knit alliance between men of strangely diverse races which was to strike some shrewd blows on the enemy's nerves along his dangerously exposed flank.

Such were the warriors with whom the fortunes of the Western Mayu V Force were to be intimately joined for the next two months as they sallied out together on their raids, night after night, the one following swiftly on the heels of the previous one. Holmes went on every one of them. Two particular operations were specifically ordered by higher command, but most other raids were entirely of his own promptings and based on the information from his scouts, the plans for each being worked out with Cartwright and, when necessary, with Binks Firbank. He did not himself command any of the expeditions, which was very properly the responsibility of the officer in charge of the troops, even if only a subaltern, but he nevertheless frequently encouraged or prompted the leadership and took a decidedly combatant part, usually giving the signal to attack by throwing the first grenade. He was fond of the quick-acting four-second grenade, an article too dangerous for the novice.

On the other hand, with the privileged exceptions of 'Jemadar' Shaffi and occasionally such men as Kaloo the Killer, he would not allow his scouts to become involved in the actual fighting and, to their regret, told them to fade away before the assaults were made. For their further protection, so that, if captured, they might possibly escape the fate of fifth columnists, he put his scouts into khaki shirts and shorts or trousers, which pleased them mightily, for it ranked them with British soldiers. For the same reason and as a very proper soldier himself, Holmes discarded his lungyi when accompanying troops into action and wore khaki drill uniform.

First Blood

The West Africans' first raid did not turn out as planned but gave Holmes a neat opportunity to pay off his lingering grudge against Dodan. A message from Habibullah at No-Can-Do brought him news that a Japanese mule-supply column was moving up towards Razabil and was expected to halt at the village of Godusara on the night of 22 January. This, thought Holmes, just suited Briggs's brief and should make a nice exercise for the West Africans. Cartwright eagerly agreed and together they made a quick plan. This was 'just the job', said Cartwright, for Angus Campbell, a young, tall, athletic, mad-keen subaltern. With ten Africans and the grinning Harpo Marx, accompanied by Shaffi, he and Holmes left Maungdaw that night in one of Firbank's steam launches, making for No-Can-Do. There, to their disappointment, they learnt from Habibullah that the enemy column had gone straight through Godusara and up into the hills.

It then occurred to Holmes that at No-Can-Do they were very nicely placed to beat up the enemy post at Dodan, which had thwarted him earlier in the month. Campbell jumped at the idea and they held a council-of-war with Shaffi and Habibullah.

This time Holmes said: 'We'll get at them from the rear. It will mean a longer walk but the blighters won't expect an attack from that side.'

Then he reminded Habibullah what had happened last time. 'The *Japani*,' he said, 'always seem to use Jiffs as night sentries while they go to sleep themselves. You lead the way, but let the jemadar do the stalking when you get nearer. He's the expert.'

The fourteen men crossed to the mainland waist-deep in water at half-tide and were soon moving over sand dunes and then open paddy. It was very cold. Barefooted, the Africans were like huge shadows, moving without a sound. So, thought Holmes, would they have looked when out on a raid in the old days of tribal wars.

Every forty yards or so across the sandy melon-fields the raiders halted and went to ground, while Shaffi and Habibullah scouted ahead. They reached Dodan, a place of few bashas but many trees, and found it deserted by the villagers, usually a sure sign that the enemy was present, for the Japanese, having begun to suspect the villagers along this coast to be helping the British, ordered them to evacuate wherever they established a post.

Soon the raiders were behind a wooden house with a corrugated iron roof and here the troops halted and went to ground, the atmosphere now tense with expectation. Shaffi, having completed his utterly noiseless reconnaissance, crept back and pointed out three enemy trenches. Campbell gave the signal to his men to surround the position and the encircling movement was completed without sound. All lay down again, waiting for Campbell's word. They were barely eight yards from the Jap trenches. Holmes, lying next to Campbell, could feel his heart thudding against the ground. When was the boy going to give the order? He nudged Campbell and whispered:

'Get on with it.'

Holmes himself threw the first grenade and the little battle erupted in violence. Grenades poured into the enemy trenches. The Japs screamed, but manned their weapons and fired rapidly at random. The flashes of their rifles were only a few yards from the Africans and bullets were whizzing everywhere. Sergeant Avunga, seeing a long Japanese rifle aimed directly at Holmes, darted instantly in front of him and took the bullet intended for Holmes.

The fireworks stopped almost as suddenly as they had started. The spurts of rifle fire from the enemy trenches ceased and several forms leaped up and ran away through the thin

African ring. A bundle in a blanket was seen wriggling stealthily along the ground. It was firmly grabbed by two Africans and turned out to be the Jiff sentry, who was quickly dispatched.

Campbell and Holmes went forward. Four Japanese were lying dead, but so also was the gallant Sergeant Avunga, of whose act of self-sacrifice Holmes was quite unaware; he knew only that the sergeant had fallen in front of him.

Documents and identifications were collected and it was time to pull out, before the enemy sent reinforcements. They made their way back quickly, six men carrying the corpse of the big sergeant, whose death his comrades keenly felt. As the steam launch had been unable to wait for their return, the party re-embarked in kistis that had been rustled up before by Harpo Marx and were paddled across to the tip of the Teknaf Peninsula, as Holmes and Shaffi had been before. Even now, however, the little expedition was not over. Campbell and his Africans were keen to have another go and Holmes was asked what other target he could offer. Possessed by the glow of magic kindled by these days of high adventure, Holmes was only too ready to agree and suggested another village near No-Can-Do called Ponra, or, interpreted, 'Monk's Village', for a pagoda stood there. It was rather a nasty little village, set about by mud and mangroves, but it was to have its place in the high adventures to come.

Accordingly, after a gigantic 'chop' of curried goat and rice provided by the friendly local people, followed by a long rest, the expedition paddled back across the Naf again that night, reached Ponra without incident and laid an ambush. But the pigeons did not appear and, after waiting in dead silence until 2 a.m., the raiders withdrew and had a stiff paddle against the tide back to Maungdaw.

The little exploit, despite the loss of their sergeant, filled the Africans with glee. The whole regiment thrilled at the news that their comrades brought back. Cartwright took a more professional interest, inquiring into every detail as a lesson for future operations. Holmes had plenty to say to him.

'As far as it went,' he said, 'it was quite a good little show, but if we go on like this we shall all get killed.'

'Go on, Denis.'

'In the first place, we weren't nearly strong enough to do the job properly. We ought to have a superiority of three-to-one for this sort of thing.'

'So all the books say, but it is not always possible; nor always right. There's something else on your mind, too, isn't there?'

'Yes, a matter of tactics. There was an awful tense pause after the grenade attack. Our experience in fighting the Japs has shown that we have got to go straight in with the bayonet immediately after the grenades. Not a moment's pause. We must swamp them before they can grab their guns.'

'The same as that dangerous pause after an artillery barrage.'

'Exactly. The Japs are damned good at that. They lie low while the high explosive is bursting but, the instant it stops, up they pop.'

'Ditto the Germans, of course. It may mean casualties from our own grenades, but that is a risk we must accept.'

Alethangyaw Overrun

A week later a far more tempting bird flew into Holmes's sights, the fattest yet, and the plot that was hatched for its discomfiture was sealed with General Briggs's special approval.

Holmes's scouts brought him word on 25 January that the enemy had mounted a gun at 'I'll thank you', with a garrison of about thirty men and machine-guns covering the beaches.

Cartwright's plan, after consultation with Holmes and Firbank, was to embark the whole of the Nigerian squadron in two of Firbank's launches, land at Alethangyaw in kistis, capture the gun, dispatch as many Japanese as possible and return by way of No-Can-Do, which would be used as a forward base.

The Nigerian squadron, led by 'Satan' Mooring, embarked at about 10 o'clock on the night of the 27th. Cartwright himself was in command and 'Binks' Firbank, not to be left out of a promising occasion, personally commanded the two little ships, which carried six large kistis. It goes without saying that Holmes was also there, accompanied by Shaffi, the mulvi Siddiq, 'Tommy-gun' and Osiullah, the fisherman who had formerly lived in Alethangyaw. Accustomed so far to hunting small game only, Holmes sensed all the exhilaration that is stimulated by going after larger and more dangerous quarry. He had begun to pick up this gameful way of thinking from Cartwright, who, in his horseman's manner, spoke of each raid as a 'chase'.

The first attempt at a landing aborted. A high surf was running when the expedition arrived off Alethangyaw at midnight. After casting off from the launches the kistis, battling against the waves on the ebbing tide, took two hours to reach the beach. Two of them were swamped. Regretfully, Cartwright called off the raid. Some fifty men went back to the launches in the remaining four kistis, leaving Holmes, Mooring and about twenty Africans stranded ashore.

They were in great danger. Enemy detachments were stationed in nearly every village. Patrols ranged many of the footpaths. Daylight was but two hours away. All were wet through and chilled to the bone. The Africans were shivering. Mooring said to Holmes:

'Where do we go from here, Watson?'

'To No-Can-Do, Satan. Quick as we can.'

Luck was with them, however. Led by Shaffi and Tommy-gun, they reached No-Can-Do at dawn and at about 8 a.m. a launch took them back to Maungdaw. Undoubtedly their withdrawal had been seen by the enemy and Holmes fully expected a warmer reception next time.

None the less, the operation was repeated on the night of 30 January and in more ambitious scope. General Briggs, now deeply committed in the grim struggle for the Razabil Fortress, was anxious that the pressure should be kept up on the coast sector. What he wanted now was a raid of such a scale as to induce the enemy to think a landing in force was being made. The plotters at Maungdaw needed no urging. Cartwright decided to commit both the Nigerian and the Gold Coast Squadrons. Fifth Division also gave him an independent Pathan commando (85th Special Service Company), under Major John Selwyn.

Furthermore, in order to give colour to the idea of a large-scale landing and in the absence of the genuine articles, a devil's symphony of all the roars and fireworks of a big battle was to be simulated by two deception officers from 15th Corps, Lt-Colonel Frank Wilson, the artist-cavalryman, and Captain

D

John Nicholson. Gun-blasts, the whistle and burst of shells, the growling of approaching tanks, coloured rockets and tracer bullets made up the major part of their infernal repertoire.

The outline plan was that Selwyn's Pathans should hold No-Can-Do as a firm base and provide protection for Wilson's 'noises off' on the mainland, while Mooring's Nigerians made the main attack on Alethangyaw and the Gold Coasters, under Alan McBean, raided the near-by Dodan once more.

As guides for this fairly considerable force of well over one hundred men, Holmes deployed a strong squad of his best scouts. He himself and Shaffi went with the Nigerians, Comer and Kaloo the Killer with the Gold Coasters, the 'black bastard', Siddiq, was at his customary place with Shattock and Harpo Marx, Habibullah and Osiullah were detailed to lend their lithe and active figures as occasion demanded. Khalique, the quaint 'Inspector', took care of the Pathans.

The night of the 30th was damp and chilly. Only a slip of a moon and the multitudinous stars ornamented the heavens. The raid went with a bang, in both senses of the term, yet ended in a partial anticlimax. The fighting spirit of the Japs had been overestimated. Scared to death by Wilson's realistic flashes and crashes and the simulated approach of tanks, the garrison at Alethangyaw fled pell-mell, taking their gun with them, but leaving behind all their kits and a half-eaten meal.

In an adjacent house, however, the Nigerians caught a suspect Burmese, who turned out to be a notorious quisling, feared by all the V Force agents, two of whom he had recently denounced to the Japs. He was taken away to be tried judicially.

Holmes urged Satan to search thoroughly for documents. 'But quickly, Satan, or they may turn on us.' The whole place reeked with the awful stench of the Jap soldiery. Holmes himself, searched the officer's basha and came away with a large handful of papers, little knowing then how valuable they were.

At Dodan there was a little killing. Kaloo the Killer practised his art and Comer dropped an enemy NCO by revolver. The rest of the detachment fled. At both positions the raiders set fire to the enemy huts and stores. As they withdrew, they heard an outbreak of artillery fire behind them and, turning round, saw that Japanese guns in the hills were furiously and accurately shelling their vacated positions. The jubilant Africans laughed uproariously, but were not so pleased when, on the return trip to Maungdaw, they were caught in a gale.

The raid thus succeeded in its primary purpose of keeping the enemy jumpy about his coastal flank. But there was a far more immediate and even more valuable dividend. For the identifications that were brought away showed that the enemy troops now stationed along the coast were no longer Tanahashi's 112th Brigade, but the 144th Brigade, which had been brought all the way from the Pacific to reinforce Hanaya's army. Tanahashi's brigade had gone the other side of the Mayu Range, in preparation for Hanaya's forthcoming '*Ha-Go*' offensive, now imminent. The information was extremely important, but unfortunately it was not properly interpreted at a higher level, with results that were soon to be painfully felt.

7

The Magic Days

'Chop Um Up' – The Ambush – The Indin 'Chase'
Pilot Officer 'Thompson'

Hanaya's offensive was launched with the utmost audacity in the early hours of 4 February and the battle that ensued dominated all activity and all thought in Arakan for the next three weeks. It was aimed primarily at Messervy's 7th Division on the farther side of the Mayu range. Hanaya's intention was to attack Messervy in the rear and destroy him by a series of hammer blows, with the Golden Fortress defences as the anvil. Then he would cross the hills and destroy 5th Division. It happened that 7th Division was then rather widely extended, on both sides of the Kalapanzin, in preparation for its own assaults on Letwedet and Buthidaung.

Hanaya's method of penetration was sensational. Under cover of the usual early morning mist, he slipped a solid column of 5,000 men, sixteen abreast, led by Mugh guides, through a narrow gap between two units of Messervy's left flank. The force was led in person by Maj.-General Tohutaro Sakurai and spearheaded by 112th Brigade under Tanahashi, who, as V Force's recent identification should have shown, had been transferred from the Western Mayu. They carried rations for only a few days, counting on seizing a large store of booty from the British.

By this bold, old-time manœuvre and precisely advised of the British positions by his Mugh informers, Sakurai penetrated six miles of British territory almost completely empty of troops. Then he wheeled left from behind Messervy and split up into four tentacles, which swung south and west in an entangling movement. One of the tentacles seized the critical pass across

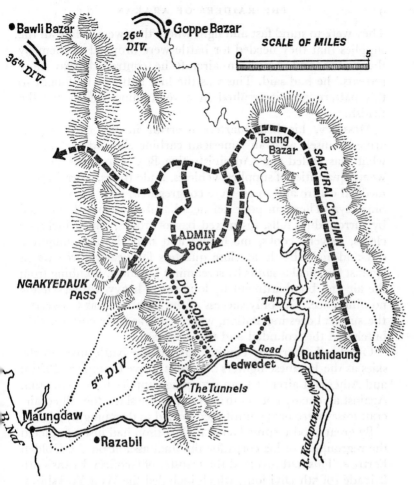

Fig. 5. 'The Battle of the Box', showing main enemy thrusts.

the Mayu hills, known as Ngakyedauk (or 'Okydoke') Pass. Seventh Division was trapped.

Then occurred one of the most remarkable battles in history. All the signs were that the disaster of the year before might be repeated. This year, however, things were different. Mount-batten had previously ordered that, when cut off in future, the troops were not to withdraw, nor try to cut their way out.

They were to stand fast and fight where they were, while all the supplies that they needed for battle were dropped to them by the British and American aircraft he controlled. 'No more retreats,' he had said. This was the first battle to be fought to this pattern and it resulted in a resounding victory for the British.

Messervy, his headquarters overrun in the early hours, armed himself with an American carbine and led the way to what was called the 'Administrative Box' two miles distant, where quantities of supplies, vehicles, mule trains, workshops, a medical centre and so on were congregated, near the village of Sinzweya. There, in poor defences hastily dug and dominated by surrounding hills, his mixed bag of troops, which included clerks, drivers, cooks, mechanics and mule leaders, fought a day-and-night battle at close quarters for nearly three weeks against fanatical assaults by screaming Japanese. Bombing from the air and bombardment by long-range heavy artillery made no difference. The only success of the Japanese was to overrun the surgical dressing station, where, as was their custom, they butchered the wounded and the doctors.

Overhead, sharp air combat carried the battle up into the skies as the Japanese fighters and guns strove to stop the British and American aircraft from dropping supplies to the garrison. Against an enemy not yet driven out of the skies, the Allied aircraft losses were heavy until they turned to dropping by night.

By great good fortune General Christison had just completed the regrouping of his corps for the final assault on the Golden Fortress. This had involved the transfer of Geoffrey Evans's 9th Brigade (of 5th Division), which included the West Yorkshires, from the Maungdaw sector to the east of the Mayu hills. They accordingly moved to Messervy's assistance from the south. And before long Lomax's 26th Division came back into their old stamping ground from the north. The encirclers were encircled. Okydoke Pass was recaptured. After three weeks the Japanese were completely outfought. Shattered, half-starving from lack of the rations that they had counted on capturing, leaving 4,600 corpses on the ground, the remnants began to creep back even before Hanaya had given leave to withdraw. For the very first time, Japanese troops began to surrender.

The 'Battle of Ngakyedauk Pass', the cumbrous title that has
been given by the official historians to this momentous battle, or
the 'Battle of the Box' in popular usage, was a terrific morale
booster to the whole of Slim's new Fourteenth Army. It had
been fought with great skill and superb courage, backed by
Mountbatten's inspired new stratagem. Holmes soon learnt that
of the all-gallant cast in the 'Admin Box' the leading heroes had
included his old friends of the West Yorkshires, who had made
endless counter-attacks, Frink's 25th Dragoons, whose Lee-
Grant tanks blasted the enemy at close range, together with
gunners of all sorts and sizes, firing point-blank in the old style
and calling upon the RAF to 'drop us some bayonets'.

At Maungdaw, as in the rest of the world, little was known
of these heroic incidents until the battle was over, but its
beginning was plainly heralded by the strong enemy air forces
that flew over the town on the first two mornings and evidence
of the combat, which quickly spread over a large area, was then
daily seen and heard at Dewdrop Inn. Shaffi and his fellow
scouts watched and listened, fascinated. The crash and blast of
gun and bomb punctuated all hours in sudden bursts of fury.
The bombers and fighters of both sides, sweeping in from
opposing directions, could be discerned over the bristly crest of
the Mayu hills, stippled with the powder-puffs of anti-aircraft
fire.

This, then, Holmes thought, was the enemy offensive that he
had been expecting. He wondered how much heed had been
paid by the Intelligence staff to the reports that had been sent
in by the V Forces – his own and that of the Eastern Mayu
under Antony Irwin (who was himself playing a gallant part in
the 'Box').

It was not until long afterwards that he learned how it had
all been disregarded by a staff too engrossed with plans for their
own offensive. This applied not only to the evidence collected
by the African raid on Alethangyaw but with even more force
to the precise intelligence jointly collected on the other side of
the hills by Anthony Irwin and the bearded 'Pirate' Edwards,
the latter now working in the Kaladan valley. A captured map,
the forward dumping of stores on the 'Pumpkin Hill' sector, the
mobilization of large gangs of Arakanese porters, the arrival of

two new field hospitals – all had been uncovered systematically, after the first small warning signs, by deep penetrations by the V Force men. The exact route was known and was gone over by Edwards. Even in their calculations of the enemy's timing he and Irwin were only a day out.

On the last day of January Irwin, weak with malaria and dysentery, hurried to 7th Division headquarters on a borrowed motor-cycle and reported personally to Frank Messervy. The general sent him at once to 15th Corps headquarters, where he was fobbed off by junior staff officers and his information ignored. Angry and in physical distress, Irwin returned to 7th Division, where the unflappable Messervy greeted him by saying: 'You were a day out, Tony; they took Taung Bazar this morning!'

The critical battle occasioned a sense of alertness throughout all forces on its fringes. Maungdaw was particularly vulnerable, especially since the departure of 9th Brigade. Enemy forces were only a little distance away to east and south. It was apprehended that they might attempt a similar penetration of 5th Division and try to capture the food and supplies in the well-stocked port. Holmes was summoned to an urgent conference of all COs by the Commandant, Colonel Jardine, in Maungdaw and found everyone looking very serious. A tight, day-and-night watch on security was ordered. Holmes was called upon to provide a section of scouts to watch the coast. A black-out was to be enforced. Every locality was to become a defended 'box' girdled with barbed wire. No movement after dark.

Such measures were very troublesome for the V Force men. Holmes said to Cartwright:

'This is a hell of a bind. It's more than ever important now that my chaps should be out and about getting all the gen they possibly can. And they've got to bring it in damned quick. But I can't possibly give them any passwords.'

Cartwright, whose Africans were garrisoning Maungdaw, replied: 'You will have to take this damned seriously, Denis. You and your scouts must just keep away from Maungdaw at night, that's all. Otherwise they'll get shot up for certain.'

Holmes went back to Dewdrop Inn thoughtfully and gave orders to his tiny establishment to dig defences. Khyber Khan at once took charge and became very much the havildar. He began to drill the unmilitary entourage, made them stand-to night and morning and enjoined them to stay at their posts till death. Slit trenches were dug and they all practised diving into them at a moment's notice. Danny, the cook, armed himself with his broad-bladed *dah* and a grenade, but Khyber took the grenade away from him. 'You will blow yourself up with that, Danu Meah, and us too,' he said.

The state of tension lasted for about ten days. The number of trained combatant troops in the town was small and Colonel Jardine's chief anxiety was the behaviour of the non-combatant ones and the civilian labour. The Royal Indian Navy appeared in the Naf and began patrolling the coast and shooting up supposed enemy positions.

To Holmes it appeared that information on enemy movements was more than ever necessary in that situation. He sent his scouts into the villages that lay to the south to call upon his agents and other informers, with due instructions to return before dark. Little of significance resulted but at the large village of Godusara, seven miles to the south, a scout learned that an enemy force of about company strength had arrived and that one of his agents there was expecting a small Japanese party to collect rice and cigarettes at his house next morning.

A prisoner would be valuable at this juncture for interrogation. Holmes, finding the state of tension at Maungdaw not to his liking, went out immediately. He could not ask for any of the Africans, who were committed to defence duties. So he took with him only Jack Comer and Habibullah, who had brought the news. But he was to be disappointed by another anticlimax.

Godusara lay some three miles from the coast. An approach by land was far too hazardous, but Holmes had taken due note of the fact that the chaungs which so bedevilled the advance of troops were a godsend for anyone who wanted to make a deep penetration into enemy country by stealth.

The three men accordingly left Maungdaw in a tiny kisti on the night of 7 February, paddled down the Naf, turned into a big, muddy chaung and stole up a small creek that took them to Godusara. Evading the enemy garrison successfully, they reached the agent's house near the creek and hid in a loft, with hand grenades ready. There, lying between baskets of rice, they watched between cracks in the flooring. The enemy collecting party duly arrived, chattering like a lot of monkeys, but, to Holmes's disgust, there were eight of them, all armed. He and Comer itched to attack them, but had ruefully to decide that 'the better part of valour is discretion'.

The chattering Japs having left, and Holmes and his scouts having come down, another scout, named Basa Meah, arrived, from whom Holmes learned that the new enemy troops at Godusara were only Jiffs. Having hidden all day, the hunters re-embarked in the kisti and safely regained the waters of the Naf, where they ran into one of those extraordinary nonsenses that occur when nerves are jittery and Rumour flaps her bat-like wings.

Quite suddenly several shells from a naval craft of some sort passed overhead and burst not far away. Supposing the fire to have been directed at themselves, they hurriedly beached the kisti and, at what might have seemed a greater risk than the naval guns, made the six miles to Maungdaw on foot, without encountering any Japs.

Arriving at 3 a.m., they were worried to find the Africans standing-to in their defence positions, very alert and expecting an attack. Fortunately Holmes was recognized and got through after a little difficulty, when he insisted on having Cartwright aroused from his bed. Cartwright looked as though he had seen a ghost and said:

'My God, Denis! I thought you were dead.'

'Dead? Where on earth did you get that idea from?'

'A signal about a couple of hours ago said that you and Comer had been captured and killed.'

'What tripe! Anyhow, what's all this flap about, Richard?'

'Fairly serious, it seems. A Japanese commando force is reported heading upriver for Maungdaw and hundreds of them are massing at Godusara for a land attack.'

'Godusara! Absolute nonsense! We've just come from there. No one there but a lot of bloody Jiffs.'

'What about the commando force? D'you know anything about that?'

'That's not the Japs' form at all, Richard. My chaps couldn't

have missed a big thing like that. All bunkum. False news
planted by the Japs. I bet the whole thing was cooked up by
that fellow Honu.'

'Well, thank God you're alive. Better go and report to
Colonel Jardine.'

This was not all. As Holmes made his way through the town
he found it almost deserted. It was the old story and reminded
him painfully of his first visit to Maungdaw nearly a year ago.
The non-combatants and the civilian labour had stampeded
and only the combatant soldiers had not flapped – the gunners
of Major Sandy Becher's battery, the sappers, the Africans and a
few more.

Even at Dewdrop Inn, Holmes found, with a shock, only
Khyber Khan, the interpreter Shaffi and the faithful 'Father
Christmas'. They were all in a slit trench, guarding the maps
and the cash box. Khyber was in position behind a Bren-gun in
complete command of the situation. All documents and photographs had been destroyed.

The next morning, as people crept back shamefacedly, there
was still no explanation of the mystery; and Holmes was
astounded to read, a few days later, a completely bogus report
of how the Royal Indian Navy had successfully intercepted a
water-borne assault on Maungdaw.

Meanwhile the Maungdaw troops patrolled actively. Ben
Grassby and Bill Bond took out a joint party of Gold Coasters
and Nigerians at night to ambush an enemy mule train at a
chaung crossing, but drew a blank. They heard splashing in
the chaung and had their fingers on the trigger, but found later
that the noises were caused by some elephants having a midnight bath. Their only prize was a not-unwilling Jiff prisoner,
who proved to be a useful source of information.

'Chop Um Up!'

As the nervous tension at Maungdaw slackened, Holmes
thought that Cartwright would be able to spare a few of his
Tarantulas for raiding parties. A very tempting fruit came into
his hands a day or two later and highly satisfactory was to be its
consumption.

A report was brought in from Baba Khan, always one of the most valuable agents, that the Japanese had mounted a section of 75-mm guns in a copse called Damankhali, close to No-Can-Do, with a protective infantry detachment of some twenty men. The information was beautifully detailed. Baba Khan had so gained the confidence of the Japanese artillery officer that he had been shown the officer's own scale plan of the position, with the layout of the gun position and trenches exactly marked. Of this Baba Khan, with perfect *sang-froid*, had made an accurate copy, which he now forwarded to Holmes by one of the scouts.

'A lovely chase,' said Cartwright when Holmes offered it to him. 'All right, we'll certainly do this one. I'll give it to the Gold Coasters and use half the squadron. You'll go too, of course, Denis.'

'Rather. I'd better lay on a few sampans, this time. Forty chaps would mean an awful lot of kistis.'

They discussed timings, tides and the method of withdrawal (always a tricky matter on a raid) and came to the conclusion that the withdrawal might have to be in daylight.

'Sampans won't do for that,' said Holmes. 'Too risky. But perhaps Binks can let us have one of his launches for the withdrawal.'

Firbank was as willing as ever and gave them Charles Cornish's *Damodar*. She was to pick them up at No-Can-Do at 6 a.m., just before dawn.

On the night of 11 February a gay party was held at Dewdrop Inn. They talked about the plan and drank to it, with the assistance of a bottle of rum produced by Jack Farquharson, one of the Rhodesians. Then they smeared themselves with the black camouflage cream, took up their weapons and made their way quietly to the sampans in the Tat Chaung.

The little flotilla cast off at 11 p.m., transporting the Gold Coasters under the command of Major Alan McBean, the other Rhodesian. As they were going to attack in four groups, Holmes gave them four of his scouts – Harpo Marx, Osiullah, Habibullah and Basa Meah. They were quickly out into the Naf, heading south for their ten-mile voyage. The moon was just past the full and rode the night huge and brilliant. The falling tide bore the sampans along at a fair speed. Strict silence all the way was the order, for noise travels far across water. The only sound was the subdued rhythmic motion of the sculls and the distant rumble of 7th Division's still critical battle. A cool sea breeze fanned their passage and the flickering flashes of the guns challenged the bright lamp of the moon. The Africans had had their usual big meal and sat contentedly, blacker than the night.

They reached No-Can-Do about 1 a.m., somewhat chilled. Their friends on the island greeted them quietly and helped them to disembark and wade ashore. Then, mustered by their officers and NCOs, the Africans listened to McBean's final orders, spoken quietly. The Damankhali Copse lay two miles away, across a stretch of mud flats and beyond the melon fields of Dodan. McBean's plan was to attack in the dawn ground-mist. One section, under himself, was to attack in the centre, two sections would come in on the left, and one section would move to the right rear as a cut-off party. All were to close in for the kill. The signal for the attack would come from Holmes, who would throw the first grenade. McBean ended by repeating the vital point:

'Grenades first. Then quick in with bayonet and chop um up one time. Savvy?'

They savvied all right. Holmes, watching them, and he himself tingling with anticipation, could sense that the big men were itching to go. The memories of thousands of years of similar raids were in their blood, separated from their consciousness by only the frailest membrane. Bareheaded and barefooted, they differed from their fathers in little else than their weapons.

There was some time to wait, but at the appointed hour the raiders formed up again and moved off in single file. They crossed the mud bank and swung to the left, each section led by its V Force scout. Holmes moved with the right section. It was an ideal night approach march, with a good moon to help.

Thirty minutes cautious marching in the sandy, slightly undulating ground brought them to a little ridge of high ground only 100 yards from the enemy. But that 100 yards was flat and completely open, devoid of cover and deadly if they were seen in the moonlight. All dropped to the ground. Ahead, against the clear night sky, loomed the black rectangles of two huts and some lesser, indeterminate shapes. The four scouts glided noiselessly forward to reconnoitre. After what seemed to be a lifetime of waiting on a knife-edge of suspense, the scouts crept back to report all well. At 5.25, obeying a hand signal from McBean, the forty waiting figures rose as one man and advanced cat-like across the open with hunched shoulders and crouching gait under a sinking moon.

Thirty yards from the objective there was another halt, where the scouts actually pointed out the enemy dispositions in detail. Now it could be seen that the two gun positions were screened by light bamboo fencing and that the huts were just behind them. No movement was to be seen, nor any sound heard. The scouts' work had been perfect. On Holmes's previous orders they then faded away ghost-like, leaving the field to the Africans as the first faint flush of light began to tint the sky beyond the hills.

The ground mist rose in dense swathes. Under its cover the hunters crept forward step by step to within eight yards of the enemy. A light appeared suddenly in the hut on the right. No doubt the cook was beginning to prepare the morning meal. At some small sound he came out of the hut, a bowl in his hand, and looked to the right.

Holmes chose this moment to give the signal for the attack. Stepping forward a few more paces he lobbed a four-second grenade at the cook. It struck him full-toss in the chest with an audible thud. The Jap started back, dropping the bowl, his face convulsed with terror. Almost instantaneously the grenade exploded and killed him.

In a matter of seconds forty more grenades were bursting in the enemy position and the gun screens torn down. The Japanese rushed pell-mell out of their bashas and the next volley of grenades caught them in the open. Even before the last fell McBean's voice was heard above the din:

'No more grenades. Give um bayonets one time! Chop um up!'

The Africans stormed in, bellowing, their blood up. The bayonets were put to their work. The Japanese still alive had leapt for their arms but at sight of the towering black figures in the misty dawn, ferocious and menacing, they screamed and ran all ways in panic after firing only a few shots. To the wild uproar was added a sickening stench of mingled blood and the sharp smoke of explosives, which roused the Africans to frenzy. In a sudden blood-lust some of them began to attack the fallen figures of the wounded and dead Japs with bayonet and machete, thrusting and slashing. A British sergeant rushed out and, himself narrowly missing the swing of a machete, closed with an African in the act. Officers roared out orders to stop the slaughter.

There was sudden silence. The Africans stood victorious on the scene. Eleven Japanese, including an officer, lay dead. Several more were wounded. McBean, a British NCO and one or two Africans had sustained slight wounds, some of which were from their own grenades so swiftly followed up. All now turned their attention to the chief prize that they hoped to carry away – the guns. Only one was to be seen, the other pit being empty. A British NCO took charge and a detachment of Africans began to haul it away with ropes found in the gun pit.

There was great glee at the capture of this trophy. The regiment believed, and probably rightly, that it was the first Japanese gun ever captured in the Burma campaign.

As soon as the gun had been dragged away and while Holmes was hunting for documents, the Japanese who had escaped began firing at the Africans with a machine-gun and small-arms from somewhere in the mist to the rear. The raiders, well-trained, at once turned, on the defensive, and an African Bren-gunner coolly got down behind his weapon. Holmes instinctively dropped beside him to keep him company. Before opening fire, the African thrust a grenade into Holmes's hands saying: 'Careful, sah, he got no pin.' It was a grenade with the safety-pin withdrawn which he had been holding tight ever since the order 'No more grenades!' Holmes hastily lobbed the dangerous object in the direction of the enemy while the Bren-gunner opened short bursts of fire.

The prompt action enabled the raiders to make a clean withdrawal under his protective fire. McBean sounded his whistle and, waving both arms, shouted: 'Get back now! Get back.' When all the others had gone, the Bren-gunner himself jumped up and doubled back, with Holmes beside him. A little

harshly, the regimental War Diary records that the raiding party
'had to evacuate at dawn and seems to have missed the chance
of a bigger killing'. It records also that the Japanese, stung
by this sharp probe, soon afterwards reinforced the position by
seventy or eighty men. But Damankhali had not seen the last
of the Tarantulas.

McBean's force withdrew through a little rearguard under
a British NCO. It was nearly full daylight. They moved in good
order at speed, doubling for short distances, taking turns at
hauling the gun and helping the wounded. The perspiration
streamed down their faces, making rivulets in the coatings of
camouflage cream. But the Africans were in the seventh heaven
of exultation, chattering like a crowd returning from a football
match and occasionally bursting out into chants that reminded
Holmes of *Sanders of the River*.

He himself, while giving an arm to McBean, was laughing
and singing 'After the Ball is Over'. Never had he felt the sense
of magic so strongly. His heart warmed towards the ebullient
Africans and to the British NCOs who had set them so splendid
an example. What was all this nonsense about the Japs' fighting
prowess?

The raiders arrived at No-Can-Do dead-tired, with parched
throats, clamouring for water as the sun rose in its strength and
the cormorants shook out their wings. There was no sign of the
Damodar, which was to take them back to Maungdaw, but they
could not blame Cornish, for he had been asked to pick them up
at 6 a.m. and it was now long past that time.

Anticipating that the Japanese would follow them up and
begin mortaring, they began to dig in, when a ship was seen to
be coming up the Naf. As she approached she was seen to be
wearing the White Ensign. All stood up on the seaward side of
the island and waved vigorously with their shirts. The ship saw
them and drew in. She was a survey ship, commanded by
Lieutenant Grattan. He took them and their captured gun on
board and the ship's company gave them a welcome in the
fashion typical of the Royal Navy.

Tea, rum, Senior Service cigarettes, sleep, bliss.

The Ambush

There was to be no rest. A series of raids now followed in quick succession. On the very afternoon of returning from the Damankhali raid Holmes had a new problem.

On arrival at Dewdrop Inn he saw two or three natives squatting outside, obviously waiting to see him. But, feeling tired, he mounted the steps of the basha and, after a cup of tea and a papaya brought to him by Khyber Khan, decided to wash, shave and go to sleep.

Shaffi and Father Christmas, however, came up and said that the men outside had some information of the utmost value. Holmes accordingly came out and found that two of the men were scouts from Alethangyaw and the third was a mere boy of about fifteen, a girlish, pale-faced creature. He gave his name as Azhar Meah. He had no relatives locally and had moved forward with the Japs from Akyab. On reaching Alethangyaw, he was interrogated by V Force scouts and, not being able to account for his presence satisfactorily, had been sent to Rob Roy for questioning. The little agent had sent him forward to Holmes, with the two scouts as escort.

Shaffi and others urged that the boy should be shot as an obvious Japanese spy. Holmes, however, felt sorry for him. He questioned him exhaustively, testing his veracity by facts and events that he himself knew and with information from other sources. He concluded that Azar Meah was telling the truth and was, indeed, too frightened to do otherwise. Among other matters he confirmed some information that Holmes had received and for which he was seeking corroboration. This was that the Japanese had set up a new post far away down the coast at Indin, where Tanahashi had dramatically burst in upon the British 6th Brigade from across the hills the year before. This accorded with other information that showed the presence of some thirty to forty Japanese in the Indin area.

Too tired to question the boy further, Holmes arranged for the Field Security staff to collect him. Shaffi was upset, still urging that the boy should be shot or else made to go in front of the next raid. Holmes replied:

'Allah is generous, Shaffi. He will guide us, as He always does. I cannot have women and children killed.'

He had touched the jemadar on the right spot. His dark eyes softened, for essentially he had a generous heart. He answered:

'If God wills, sahib, he will bless us.'

'As God wills, Shaffi.'

Though Indin was nearly thirty miles away, a raid was laid on the very same night and Holmes, shaking off his fatigue, would not be left out. It was the longest haul yet attempted. Firbank lent them *Yengyua* and two Fleming barges and the Royal Indian Navy gave them Motor Launch 441 for company.

Cartwright himself commanded this time but the raid was a flop. There was a high surf, one of the heavy barges grounded and only one weak patrol could be put ashore. The Africans were disappointed but Holmes said: 'Never mind, we'll have another go soon.'

The long Okydoke battle was now, in the middle of February, at about its climax. The Japanese had been severely shaken by what Hanaya called the 'hysterical resistance' of the British, but the issue was still in the balance. Both 5th and 7th Divisions were heavily engaged and offensive operations on the western sector had halted. The garrison of Maungdaw, however, were enjoying a quiet time in brilliant weather. The sun was hot, the sky deep blue, the river sparkling. Holmes and the Tarantula officers went bathing and fishing from a Fleming barge. The Sierra Leoneans of C Squadron, commanded by Major Jack Stokes, arrived from India. Holmes himself entertained nightly at Dewdrop Inn, and Khyber Khan, from sources that Holmes refrained from prying into, served up the most delicious dishes cooked by Danu Meah.

A day or two afterwards Richard Cartwright called at Dewdrop Inn and found Holmes naked to the waist in a green lungyi, thoughtfully going through some recent reports from his scouts. He asked: 'Anything interesting, Denis?'

'Quite interesting. This stuff I've been sorting out is about a new Jap post at Kanyindan. It looks a very nice "chase" and I think we ought to do it.'

'Kanyindan? But that's only the other side of Maungdaw and we're in it.'

'This is another Kanyindan, near Alethangyaw, just a small village. It means "A Row of Wood-oil Trees", which are "kanyins".'

'There seem to be a hell of a lot of Jap positions round about Alethangyaw.'

'Yes, there are. Nice and handy for good old No-Can-Do.'

'Well, what's the form at this place?'

'There's a Jap detachment of about a dozen chaps there. At night they man a position in the open paddy-fields to the west of the village and by day they retire to a group of bashas in the northern part to snooze. They have kicked out the locals from the whole of the village.'

'What are they up to, d'you think?'

'I can only suppose it's in case we attempt a night penetration. Most of the posts around there are manned by day only.'

'What's the position like?'

'A pretty tough one, on the face of it. The bunkers they occupy at night are strongly made and beautifully camouflaged and my chaps say that they blend in with the countryside so well that it's impossible to pick them out at fifty yards.'

'What's the strength of your information, Denis?'

'Pretty reliable, as far as the movements of the Japs go. We've been watching the place carefully and I've just been sorting out some new reports which tally nicely with what we've had before.'

'Sounds to me too risky for a night attack, I'm afraid, and I've no intention of doing it in daylight.'

'Quite so, Richard. Can't attack the bunkers. But, let's see, now . . .'

'What's on your mind?'

'What's come into my mind is that we might occupy the village at night, when it's empty, and beat 'em up when they come back from the bunkers in the morning.'

'H'm. That's a saucy idea. Don't they leave anyone in the village at night? No cook? No sentry?'

'My chaps say not.'

'Damned slack on their part. What sort of a place is this Kanyindan?'

'Tuppenny-ha'penny village close to the north bank of the Alethangyaw Chaung. Lots of sandy mud. Becomes an island at high tide, but a track leads from there to Alethangyaw. Lots of trees in and about the village.'

'All right, Denis, the chase is on. Let's get to work on the plan.'

Cartwright decided to command this operation himself. Mooring and his Nigerians were to make the main attack on the Kanyindan position. At the same time a small diversionary attack was to be carried out by 'Tiny' Lyons, a big, strapping Irish Guardsman of the Sierra Leone Squadron, accompanied by John Comer, on a village a mile and a half farther inland.

The Kanyindan raid was put in on the night of 16/17 February and went without a hitch. The night was moonless and the weather now much warmer. They made the trip to No-Can-Do by kisti. From there Mooring's main assault party, accompanied by Holmes and guided by Shaffi, took a circuitous route, marching part of the way along a slimy chaung that gave them good cover, and sneaked into Kanyindan from the rear at about 4.30 a.m. Their information had been sound; the little hamlet, heavily embowered in trees, was empty. Before daylight they were all ready in their ambush positions.

Lieutenant Reid Ross, a stocky, rugged Scot, with a Bren-gun and two riflemen, were in the Japanese cookhouse. A similar detachment, commanded by Sergeant Houston, was on their right, nicely concealed behind some dummies that the Japanese used for bayonet practice in their habitual manner everywhere. In the centre, Satan Mooring and Holmes were behind two large mango trees with a few riflemen. To the rear was a third Bren-gun team to deal with any Japs that might get away or with any reinforcements that might arrive.

The trap was complete and the Japanese walked into it at daylight. Draped in blankets and trailing their rifles in a slipshod manner, a dozen sleepy figures appeared walking towards the village from their trenches. The hunters let them get to within ten yards and then Holmes rolled a grenade along the ground to the feet of the first man, like a 'sneaker' at cricket. So astonished was the Jap that he bent down to see what it was and was killed instantly.

The Africans' Brens and rifles awoke to instant life and in a moment three more Japs fell dead. The remainder turned and ran back to their trenches, whence, with no little determination, they returned the fire. For a few minutes it looked as though they might get away with it, for Mooring was very properly not disposed to risk an open assault. Bullets were thudding into the mango trees behind which he and Holmes and the riflemen were partly concealed.

Then, from his post among the bayonet dummies, Sergeant Houston moved his position slightly and got his Bren-gun well sighted. An accurate burst of fire was followed by silence from the enemy.

To find out if any of them were still alive, Holmes began calling out the few Japanese phrases that he had learnt, such as 'Throw down your arms and stand up.' He was answered by angry yells. Holmes got very excited, itching to dash forward, and the calmer Mooring kept pulling him down under cover.

Another short silence and then the only two Japs who still appeared to remain alive suddenly leapt from their trench and began to run hell-for-leather southwards for the dead ground of the Alethangyaw Chaung.

On this, Mooring's great Nigerian orderly, Yaro, let out a bellow and charged after them. He swiftly overtook them and, yelling with delight, finished off each in turn with the bayonet.

Well pleased with the success of the brisk little operation, the raiders came out into the open and began to examine the bodies for documents. One African cut the ears off a dead Jap and said: 'Me give um to de Colonel for present.'

All was not yet over, however. Shaffi suddenly pointed up into a straw rick and said to Holmes:

'Sahib, *Japani* sniper.'

Holmes and Mooring looked up cautiously and saw the fellow in his peaked cap, looking as though he was trying to bury himself in the straw; probably a look-out who had gone to sleep. Ordered to come down in three languages, he did so at the third attempt and jumped down, half defiant, half apprehensive. Holmes wanted to take him alive, but even as he shouted 'No shoot' an African put a bullet in the Jap's thigh. Luckily the wound was not serious and they took him back alive, after all, the first they had captured. He was a filthy creature, covered in sores, but any prisoner was then a rarity and quite an important prize.

Before they left Kanyindan, in jubilation, the raiders set fire to the bashas that had been occupied by the Japanese and to one or two others nearest to the trenches. It was not a necessary act but the leaping flames were a symbol of triumph and the customary finale of an oriental raid. The memory of the burning was to come back to them on another fiery night on a sharper occasion.

On the march back to No-Can-Do the prisoner, in the manner common to them all before the rot set in, repeatedly begged to be killed. Yaro was eager to let him have his way. Fierce in battle, Yaro was a mountain of childish good humour at other times, with a grin like the pithy side of a grapefruit. Holmes gathered that he had had some fifteen years of service, but was still only a trooper, for, whenever he got promoted, he celebrated too freely and found himself in the guardroom ecstatically drunk, but next morning minus his stripe.

Holmes entered in his diary that night: 'The Africans are bastards for killing and I had the greatest difficulty in keeping my prisoner alive.' They all studied the unprepossessing fellow closely. Of the many Japs whom Holmes saw at different times, few ever had clean clothes or possessed any change of underwear. They were avid scribblers and carried note-books and diaries, together with visiting cards, many photographs, a silk scarf and national flag. All were wealthy in the Japanese paper money with which Burma had been flooded. There were usually a few water-sterilizing tablets and some quinine pills, the Japanese having now almost a monopoly of the world's supply of quinine. His food supplies consisted of rice, dried fish and usually some beef.

Tiny Lyons's little diversionary raid on Thandaywa went well and fulfilled its purpose; one Japanese was killed and three wounded.

The Indin 'Chase'

One night's rest and then out again.

These night affrays, in addition to their physical efforts,

incurred strong emotional strains: the tension of waiting with throbbing pulses, the anxiety about the validity of the plan, the constant watchfulness for the unexpected, the hot excitement of the conflict. When the nervous tensions have passed a feeling of irresistible drowsiness supervenes. To Holmes the feeling was similar to that experienced after a number of parachute jumps, as he was to realize when he later became a parachutist. Yet the thrill of another hunt overcame all. 'Increase of appetite had grown by what it fed on' and the gleam of magic drew him on.

He had little chance now to give way to drowsiness. The Intelligence staff at 15th Corps was anxious to know whether the enemy might be moving up new reinforcements from Akyab and orders accordingly filtered down to Holmes to secure some identifications as far south as he could. He thought that Indin, where the new enemy post reported by young Azar Meah and attacked unsuccessfully the week before, would meet the case and he put the proposition to Cartwright.

Indin had become a desolate village and the surrounding paddy-fields, once so orderly, were beginning to become overgrown with jungle. Wherever they went in Burma the Japanese made no attempt whatever to repair or alleviate the ravages of war and were wholly indifferent to the privations and difficulties of the local population. Everything that they did not need for the army was allowed to go to rack and ruin. Even the gardens of Government House in Rangoon had become a jungle.

At Indin, however, there was one good building in habitable condition. It lay some distance from the village and about a few hundred yards from the gleaming white beach. It was now tenanted by a small detachment of Japanese, who had dug some trenches outside it. As we have seen, Indin was far beyond the usual beat of the raiders, well out on the shore of the Bay of Bengal, and careful thought was given to all the information available by Holmes, Cartwright and Firbank.

Cartwright gave the 'chase' to the Nigerians and led it himself. Quite a different approach march was chosen this time, on account of the distance. Instead of making straight for the target area, the raiders, to the number of about twenty-four, took passage on 19 February with Firbank in his *Torotua* to a lovely and utterly peaceful tropical island of palms and white

sand in the picture-postcard style, right out in the Bay of
Bengal. This was Coconut Island or, more officially, St Martin's
Island, which was completely untouched by the war. The little
ship dropped anchor off shore until dark, then steamed the
eighteen miles across the bay to Indin under a small crescent
moon. There Firbank landed them safely on a beach in dead
ground about a mile from their objective.

The little operation was flawless. The Japanese had learnt no
lessons from the abortive raid of a week before and no one was
on guard. The raiders, now expert in these matters, landed
from a Fleming barge in dead silence and unobserved. There
was no surf to speak of. Cartwright himself took charge of a small
beachhead and the little assault party of twelve, guided by
Muhammad Bux, glided off like ghosts in single file over the
white sand dunes and past the leaning palms in the raw cold of
the night mist under the command of Lieutenant Hugh Burgess.
Holmes, rejoicing in the 'lovely smell of the sea', prompted
him throughout and Jemadar Shaffi trod watchfully a little in
front.

Muhammad Bux led them straight to the building, which
was surrounded in the same skilful silence. Shaffi then crept
forward to look through a window. He came back to report that
four Japs were sitting in the main room eating their supper.
There should have been more than that number, but four would
more than suit the purpose of the expedition. It was again for
Holmes to give the signal for the attack and he was satisfied. He
closed up, found one of the Japs singing a song and bowled him
the first grenade. A volley of grenades followed. The Japs leapt
up, scrambling to escape, but in a few seconds all were dead or
dying as the grenades burst with shattering effect in the
confined space. Holmes and Burgess, revolvers in hands, crashed
in at once, the Africans on their heels, but there was no need for
the bayonet. Burgess took a flesh wound from one of his own
grenades. Identifications, in the forms of pay-books and letters,
together with a Japanese flag, were collected and gathered in a
haversack and the raiders cleared out, leaving behind some
cartons of American K rations by way of deception.

However, as was suspected, not all the enemy had been
disposed of. As the raiders left the building, they were fired on by

rifles from the adjacent trenches. Most of the bullets went wide, but unfortunately one of them struck Shaffi in the leg. His comrades had to carry him the rest of the way back, but he only smiled his infectious smile and said: 'It is nothing, major sahib. Allah is great and He will call me when he wants me. Until then we will go on killing *Japani*. Allah be praised.'

Otherwise unscathed and having completed a model raid, but feeling very cold and wet, all hands were glad to be aboard the *Torotua* again and Binks, full of congratulations, was presented with the Japanese flag as a trophy for his wardroom. For Holmes not the least satisfactory feature was the accuracy of the information sent him by his agents and the boy Azar Meah. As for Shaffi, he made light of his wound, which was treated for him by Captain Nicholas, the V Force doctor, who happened to be then at Maungdaw, and he was limping about quite nimbly in a day or two.

Pilot Officer 'Thompson'

By this time – 20 February – the 'Battle of the Box' was nearly over. The next day Okydoke Pass was re-opened. The attack on 7th Division had been broken. Sakurai's stupefied columns were reeling and crawling out of the battle. Never had there been such a rout of Japanese forces. Prisoners were becoming cheaper. V Force scouts from Irwin's side of the hills were bringing in quantities of minor equipment left by the enemy: swords, flags, arms, documents, scribblings and maps, all of which were sent back to the Intelligence staff.

On the Maungdaw front operations were still stagnant, but the British forces felt forward a trifle and the Tarantulas established a standing patrol as far south as Godusara. The Sierra Leonians carried out a brilliant ambush near there, killing twelve enemy and wounding many more. Denis Holmes was having a quiet cup of tea one day with Shaffi, Siddiq and Father Christmas, when one of them remarked how much more successful the British forces might have been in the First Arakan campaign if only they had had better information of Japanese movements, such as V Force was now helping to provide. 'Last year,' said Father Christmas very correctly, 'it was

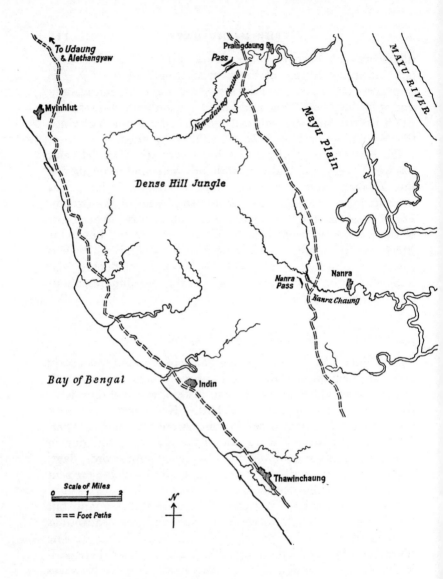

Fig. 6. Exploits farther South.

the *Japani* who seemed to know what was going on, while the British were fighting with their eyes closed.'

'He is right, sahib,' Shaffi chimed in. 'If we had been here last year, we should have been able to tell the British how the enemy had garrisoned Donbaik and built that fortress which stopped the British.'

Siddiq made a quotation from the *Koran* and added sombrely: 'Because of our past wickedness, Allah was not with us then, but He is with us now and we shall drive away these infidels.'

A quiet chorus of *Inshallah*, in which Holmes joined, greeted the mulvi's wisdom.

It was not very far from Donbaik that the eyes of Holmes and his scouts were now unexpectedly drawn. Three days after the return from Indin Hashim Boli, a trusted scout who had lived up in the hills far down the Akyab Peninsula, arrived at Dewdrop Inn with news that a RAF pilot said to be named 'Thompson' was in trouble at a village three miles south of Indin named Thawin Chaung ('The Creek of the Thawin Trees'). He had been obliged to bale out from his aircraft and was trying to make his way up to the British lines. The local Chittagonians were giving him food and shelter, but at some peril to themselves and Japanese patrols were out searching for him. He was now in close hiding near the mouth of the chaung.

Now the rescue of RAF pilots was not a V Force job, and this would be a perilous one, for the village was some twenty-eight miles down the coast in country very firmly held by the Japanese. Strictly speaking the rescue was a RAF responsibility, but Holmes knew that the RAF could do little about it and, in any case, they would need V Force help. Quick action was essential and Holmes decided instinctively to make the mission his own.

At once he sent Hashim Boli back to Thompson with a message hidden in a bamboo stick, saying that help was on the way and telling him to stay where he was. Then he set about organizing a rescue party for the next night. From Richard Cartwright he obtained a squad of Africans under John Mitra, the mortar officer of B Squadron, and from the Royal Indian Navy two motor launches, one of which was to take a medical party to a near point on the Teknaf Peninsula.

The rescue party, towing a landing craft, left on the moonless night of the 24th, but the expedition ended unhappily. When they arrived at the mouth of the chaung they found a high surf running. Holmes, Mitra and a few Africans transferred to the landing craft under the command of a midshipman; but, as they approached shore, or thought that they were so doing, the surf became worse and worse and the midshipman said that he could not risk getting the craft through. Upon which Holmes said to Mitra:

'Very well, John, we'll swim.'

The night was pitch-black, but the two officers, accompanied by Hashim Boli and one or two Africans, donned Mae Wests and jumped into the boiling surf. They suffered a tremendous buffeting but struggled on when they got a footing and found the water getting shallower. Suddenly, however, it began to get deeper again, for they had been put down not on the beach, but on a sandbank. The little party was quickly scattered. Holmes and Hashim were swept away by the swift current and Hashim was never seen again.

Holmes, obliged to jettison his tommy-gun and grenades, called out, but was not heard above the roar of the surf. His Mae West kept him afloat, but he felt himself drifting. Flashes of phosphorescence glittered all round in the dark. Quite calmly he thought: 'What ought I to do if I get carried out to sea?' Then he caught sight of the luminous dial of his watch on his wrist and thought: 'Well, if you can keep going, so can I.' At this moment the dark shape of the landing craft loomed up and he heard a voice shouting:

'Are you there, sir?'

He was hauled on board, more than half-drowned and very sick. Oddly, his first reaction when he had partially recovered was an acute embarrassment at finding himself completely naked. His next was to ask the midshipman:

'What about Thompson? Have you got him?'

'No go, sir, I'm afraid.'

'Where's Hashim?'

'Haven't found him yet, sir.'

Mitra, hauled aboard just before Holmes, had suffered a somewhat similar ordeal, but his main concern as he recovered from his bout of sickness was for the loss of his tommy-gun. 'The CO,' he said to Holmes, 'will give me a hell of a rocket.'

For another half-hour they searched for the missing scout, without success, and then sadly made their way back to Maungdaw. Holmes was very despondent at the loss of a very good scout. But he was not to be put off from his intention to rescue Thompson and at once organized another party, which set off the very same night. This time he took a squad from the Pathan commando under Captain Billy Sturrock in one of Binks's ancient launches captained by Maurice Budd. They landed safely on the night of the 25th, but had no luck, as they found that Thompson had unwisely, in the words of Holmes's diary, 'sugared off'.

So, on his return to Dewdrop Inn, Holmes delegated to John Comer the dangerous mission of going out into the villages on foot in an attempt to discover where the pilot had gone. Finally, Cartwright sent Tiny Lyons down to the creek with a patrol of Sierra Leonians, only to learn from the local V Force that Thompson had been captured.

Some time afterwards Holmes wrote in his account of operations: 'We never learnt of Thompson's subsequent fate, but I hope he will understand that V Force did their best.'

8

Screwdriver

*The Screw is Turned – The Marines Drive Inland
5th Commando Sees Them Off – Saving the Guns*

March strode in with fiery breath. A visible heat haze shim-
mered and throbbed on the sea. The mud flats stank. On shore
men wore the minimum of clothes, their bodies streaming with
rivulets of perspiration. The scorched earth became dehydrated
and its churned-up dust hung in the torrid air in motionless
clouds and laid a heavy veneer over everything. Trees, their
leaves unable to perform their functions, drooped disconsolately
under the dirty grey coating. The nights, however, lost their
chill dampness and the early mornings were no longer enveloped
in mist.

Holmes had felt some anxiety about the little community of
fishermen on No-Can-Do, fearing Japanese reprisals. He had
therefore evacuated most of the families from the little place,
but had left his section of scouts. The precaution was taken only
just in time, for the Japs raided the island on the day before the
attempt to rescue 'Thompson'. They shot it up at random and
burned down the bashas but found it empty, for the scouts,
warned by their own Intelligence Service, had escaped safely in
their boats. With a stupidity that they often showed in these
operations, the Japanese made no attempt to establish a
preventive detachment on the island.

Accordingly, on the first day of March, Cartwright sent Alan
McBean and half his squadron of Gold Coasters there to
provide a permanent garrison, and Holmes re-established his
section of scouts. McBean dug in at once and was soon being
mortared from the mainland and shelled by a 75-mm gun that

the Japs had sited at Kanyindan. Unperturbed, the Tarantulas hit back on 4 March by carrying out a devastating private raid of their own, led by Lieutenant Dick Spurrier, on the strong Damankhali position, where they killed an officer and six men and captured a machine-gun.

And now larger events began to affect the fortunes of the Western Mayu V Force. Holmes received orders to warn all the inhabitants along the coastal strip to expect heavy air bombardments early in May and that they should either evacuate their villages or else make sure that their air-raid shelters were in good order. This Holmes hated doing and recorded in his diary 'Bad show'. What on earth did we want to bomb these harmless and friendly villagers for? He did not know the reason until long afterwards, and meantime it made the work of V Force more difficult; relations with the villagers and with the scouts themselves were affected.

The signs soon began quietly to multiply that something was brewing. As soon as the Battle of the Box was over, 5th and 7th Divisions had regrouped to go straight over to the offensive again. The two outer baileys of the Golden Fortress – Razabil and the Ledwedet-Buthidaung bastions – were to be assaulted and then the two divisions were to close in swiftly to the tunnel mouths and to the great keep above and beyond. Briggs was to crack open Razabil by sending Warren's 161st Brigade on a circuitous night march from Maungdaw to attack it from the rear in a hammer-and-anvil battering. The 9th Brigade, now commanded by the tall, spare and popular figure of Brigadier 'Sally' Salomons, had come back to the territory of 5th Division after their spirited part in the Battle of the Box and were spread out to protect the southern flank of Warren's battalions, with the West Yorkshires in the scrubby foothills south-east of Maungdaw.

Briggs's anxiety was that the enemy's 144th Brigade, on the coast, might be hurried up to interfere with him. He therefore wanted to create a serious threat to the enemy's coastal flank by a seaborne landing in some strength, not a mere tip-and-run raid. For this purpose he was given some new troops of the finest mettle and, to lend verisimilitude to the threat, Japanese positions adjacent to the villagers were probably going to be bombed from the air.

Holmes, to his great regret, had just parted from John Comer, who had been recalled to his regiment, and had moved Dewdrop Inn to Karipara, just south of Maungdaw. On the same day, 5th March, he and Richard Cartwright, to their great surprise, were ordered to cross the river to Jackson's Jetty at Teknaf, where they met Brigadier 'Growler' Nonweiler, of the Royal Marines, and Captains Rylands and McGregor, of the Royal Indian Navy. Something big was obviously in the wind. Nonweiler, good-looking, square-rigged, was the commander of 3rd Special Service Brigade, better known by its later name of 3rd Commando Brigade.

From him they learnt that the Tarantulas were to come under his command for an important operation, in which V Force also would be closely involved. Cartwright and Holmes were both excited at the news and, from the outline information that Nonweiler then gave, Holmes had an idea why, in the last few days, he had been required by 5th Division to send in detailed reports on enemy dispositions at Alethangyaw and elsewhere.

They learnt also that the Commando Brigade (as we shall continue to call it) was a mixed formation of Royal Marine and Army units. Two of these – 1st (Army) Commando and 42nd Royal Marine Commando – were absent, having been delayed in their passage to India by damage to their ships from enemy submarines or aircraft. The remaining units, now on the Teknaf Peninsula, were 5th (Army) Commando, under Lt-Colonel David Shaw, a purposeful and thrusting leader, and 44th Royal Marine Commando, led by the tall and strongly built Lt-Colonel Cyril Horton.

Holmes, when later he met these units, was tremendously impressed. Never had he seen such fit young men as those who were wearing, with their jungle-green uniform, the now famous green beret. Alert, full of ardour, trained to a hair and well disciplined for battle, they had the advantage over the Africans of a higher intelligence and personal resourcefulness. The marine commando prided itself in its prowess at football, having several professional footballers in its ranks. Each commando was organized, not in companies and platoons, nor in squadrons and troops, but in 'troops' and 'sections', the total strength of each commando being about 465 all ranks. A Troop numbered sixty-five officers and men; 5th Commando designated their Troops by numerals, the marines by letters.

The Army commando had had a little seasoning at the capture of Madagascar, but the marines had never yet been in action and both, having been training on the plains in India, had no knowledge of the very peculiar conditions, possibly unique in the world, of the Arakan coast, so cut up with innumerable chaungs. Holmes thought that they looked like a bunch of super schoolboys mad-keen for a needle football match.

A few days later he took some of his leading scouts to introduce them to the commandos. Siddiq, looking more formidable than ever, was loath to leave his Nigerian Muslims, but Jemadar Shaffi, Harpo Marx, Osiullah and Habibullah felt a closer affinity with the eager and lively young British soldiers than they had with the *hubshi*. The Tarantulas were cheerful giants, good at killing the yellow infidels, but they lacked the social touch of Thomas Atkins and His Majesty's Jollies, who, with their sure instinct for native peoples, would say to them: 'Come and sit down, Johnny, and have a fag.' The scouts attached to the marines quickly became known as 'the Marx Brothers'. Each unit was also allotted a small detachment of the uniformed Burma Intelligence Corps, who, in the operations to come, did good service, especially as interpreters on the actual battlefield.

The plan for the big operation was disclosed on 8 March at a conference which Nonweiler held in the immaculate setting of Cartwright's tented headquarters under the big mangoes south of Maungdaw, with the noises of battle as background. Holmes sniffed at once the businesslike air – formal, brisk, quiet – that replaced the more easy-going plotting of 'the brotherhood'. The operation, under the code name of 'Screwdriver', was to be launched on the night of 11 March, when 5th Division would be making its vital assault on Razabil. Its purpose was to dominate the whole coastal strip inland from Alethangyaw up to the foothills of the Mayu Range, in order to prevent the enemy's reinforcements and supplies from reaching the Razabil sector and to forestall any counter-attack after the capture of Razabil;

this meant, in particular, commanding the tolerably good track that skirted the foothills and another that ran through the middle of the plain from Alethangyaw northwards. Thus the intention was not merely to launch a raid but to seize ground and hold it.

The method by which this was to be done was for the Royal Marine commando to establish a beachhead just south of Alethangyaw, capture that village and cross the coastal plain to a designated hilltop some three miles farther inland. The Africans were to provide a flank guard by capturing the Kanyindan position, now much strengthened and including a gun, and by holding a small road-bridge just south of Lamba-guna, well ahead of Cree's West Yorkshires and the other units of 9th Brigade. The Army commando was to be in reserve and to take over from the marines after a few days. V Force was to co-operate closely by providing guides for all units and by keeping them informed of enemy dispositions.

For once Holmes had no large part to play in the conference. Apart from answering some questions about the enemy, he was a mute spectator. But inwardly he was not happy about the plan. The essence of the Africans' successes so far had lain in surprise, taking the enemy from the rear or in flank in silence and clearing out quickly. The marines would no doubt take Alethangyaw all right, but there could be little chance of surprise in the subsequent advance across the plain, studded with enemy detachments; and, if they got to the hills, they would still have to be maintained and to evacuate their casualties. Furthermore, could either the Africans or the marines hold their captured positions for a protracted period against counter-attacks, without artillery support?

There was a great deal for everyone to do in a very short time. Holmes paid a quick visit to Chris O'Hara, of the West Yorkshires, to inquire of their needs, then he took out a party of senior officers of 9th Brigade, headed by Sally Salomon, on a tour of the sensitive fringe of villages on the flank of the coming battle and detailed a section of his scouts for attachment to the brigade. Then, with a pre-battle tingle in the air, he made a quick trip by kisti downriver to McBean at No-Can-Do, which was being mortared, and from there, accompanied by Shaffi,

paid a secret visit to Rob Roy at Alethangyaw to get the latest
'gen', dodging the Japanese soldiery. He returned, in very rough
weather, to Dewdrop Inn at 3 a.m. on the 11th, to find a terrific
din going on as 5th Division began its bombardment of Razabil.

That same night he set out to play his part in 'Screwdriver'.

The Screw is Turned   *164534*

There was no call for Holmes himself to go, any more, indeed,
than on any of the raids, as a combatant. His duties were to
provide information, scouts, boats and so on. But he was
damned if he was going to miss the opportunity of being in on
such a big occasion, even if this time he was going to be only a
supernumerary. Others might hurl the first grenade, fire the
first shot and lead the break-in, but he could still have a great
joy-ride and play the simple part of a fighting soldier. So he
elected to go with the Africans, with whom he felt a close
attachment and to march with his great friend Satan Mooring,
taking Jemadar Shaffi with him as usual, and feeling entirely
happy at the prospect of going into battle again with such tried
comrades.

Richard Cartwright's plan for his regiment's part in the
battle was very shrewd and a neat example of his tactical
originality. He entrusted the main attack on Kanyindan to
Mooring's Nigerian squadron, while he himself intended to
establish a command post at Dodan, now known from the V
Force to be free of the enemy, and there he proposed to mount
the heavy mortars under Purdy and John Mitra. Now Dodan
was a short mile to the west of Kanyindan, whereas Mooring
would be attacking from approximately the east. The value of
this stratagem was very soon to be apparent. The defence of the
Lambaguna bridge in the Nigerions' rear was entrusted to the
Sierra Leone squadron under Jack Stokes.

Cartwright and the mortars set out by sea for No-Can-Do
with Habibullah as their scout, but, as the marines were also to
find, there was a high surf, so that the kistis and sampans were
swamped and washed ashore. Undeterred, the big men took up
their heavy loads on their heads and their shoulders and
silently pursued their way on foot over land and mud and

chaung, reaching Dodan on time. The Nigerian assault troops, however, contrary to the Tarantulas' usual practice, were required to approach their target by land. This meant a march of twelve miles, the last two miles of which would be through territory occupied by scattered enemy detachments. Mooring divided his march into two stages. To the number of some fifty, with Hugh Burgess and Reid Ross as the two troop leaders, they paused about half-way at Gyingyaung ('Ginger Creek'), a small, depressing village with a pagoda, set among ginger bushes, recently occupied by the Japs. Here Holmes joined them and moved Dewdrop Inn forward to the village to be nearer to the scene of the new operations.

Shaffi, following his usual custom, wanted a guide who was intimate with the country that they would have to traverse that night and the village headman produced a bright and eager new scout in Fazal. The young man declared that he was 'ready to do anything that the sahib required', but asked that he might be provided with a revolver for his own protection. Holmes had none to give him, but pleased him mightily when he procured him a rifle instead.

At Ginger Creek the squadron lay up quietly all through the fierce heat of the 11th, resting among the buzz of flies, while parrots and pigeons flew languidly from branch to branch and the vivid butterflies fluttered among the ginger bushes and the papayas under a cobalt sky. The evening drew on. The myriad frogs began their nightly chorus and the tuk-tu lizard barked as the sun began to sink in splendour in the Bay of Bengal. Expectation hovered impatiently in the air. Holmes, having been entertained by the headman to a lavish dinner and sent on his way with a fervent 'Allah be with you', joined Mooring. The Africans had had a big 'chop' and fell in quietly. Their arms, equipment and water bottles were closely inspected. British NCOs were in charge of a wireless set, but it was not to be used until a chosen moment. At the word of command from Mooring the squadron turned southwards, forming into single file, guided by Shaffi and Fazal. In addition to the V Force men, a small detachment from the Burma Intelligence, under Lieutenant 'Bobby' Than Myaing, marched with them.

The moon was at the full, but its direct light would be hidden behind the mass of the Mayu hills until about 2 or 3 a.m. Thus there was a wall of darkness on their left but the way they trod was sufficiently lighted by the myriad stars. The flat countryside was silent and shuttered, except for the distant growls of the main battle and the occasional howl of a questing jackal, or, under a light breeze, the rustling of the betel-palm leaves and the creak and crackle of the bamboos as they jostled each other in their tall thickets. The squadron marched noiselessly, alert for any Japanese patrol that might be prowling around. The stars, the dead-black shadows and the trees were the only witnesses of their march. After an hour or so Holmes, looking at his watch, remarked to Mooring: 'Cyril Horton's Jollies ought to be landing soon now.'

Soon Fazal led them off into devious, untrodden ways. He took them along the banks of open paddy-fields, tinted lavender-grey in the starlight, past ghostly clusters of palms and kanyins, across muddy, unbridged chaungs and through the low scrub of untilled land where strangers would have been hard put to find a way. They were getting very near the enemy now and moved with great caution and in utter silence. When they were but half a mile or so from the enemy an awkward obstruction faced them.

Passing through the scrub, they were confronted by the broad Ton Chaung, its water glistening like polished steel and looking strangely forbidding. Here Shaffi halted the column and whispered to Holmes: 'Sahib, Fazal says it is very deep; right up to the chin.' On Mooring's orders, every man stripped and waded across, carrying his clothing and equipment on his head, an exercise to which the Africans, but not the British, were entirely accustomed.

Having crossed, the column proceeded with increased caution, halting about every hundred yards while Shaffi and Fazal reconnoitred ahead. Following a circuitous route, they came upon Kanyindan from the rear. In the grey night the village, its black shape compact and heavily wooded, seemed to their watching eyes like a sombre ghost-town, embodying who-knows-what dark secrets. They knew that, on enemy orders, it was empty of civilians, but some Japanese might well have been lurking there. They knew also that the enemy works consisted of a gun pit and two mutually supporting infantry bunkers.

The squadron halted at some distance away, listening and watching. The Africans sat, rifles between their knees, motionless. No light or movement was to be seen in the village. They could discern the charred remains of the huts that had been burnt down in the earlier raid and in imagination could smell the ashes of their burning. Away on their left they could distinctly hear the crackle and chatter of the marines' battle at 'I'll-thank-you' and knew that the garrison of Kanyindan must therefore be on the alert.

At a sign from Holmes, sitting besides Mooring, Shaffi and Fazal crept forward. They reached the perimeter of the village and then were lost to view, but Holmes knew that they were making for the farther side, where the gun position was. He was filled with admiration not only for their nerve but also for the skill with which they moved. A long half-hour of waiting had to be endured, with eyes and ears alert in all directions, arms ready for instant use. The obedient Africans sat as immobile as logs.

Almost unseen, the two scouts reappeared. Shaffi lay down and whispered to Holmes:

'Sahib, there is no one in the village and the *Japani* are all in their bunkers. I could smell them strongly. Allah be praised, sahib, the moment has come.'

Shaffi's magic smile gleamed in the moonlight and Holmes, in this tense time of waiting, was moved emotionally by the faithful scout's courage and coolness. He put a hand on Shaffi's shoulder and said:

'Good show, Shaffi. Allah is indeed with us tonight.' Then turning to Mooring he whispered:

'All set now, Satan. Let's decide what's to be done.'

According to their normal form they would have followed Shaffi silently in the dark until they were within grenade range, but tonight there were difficulties, which had, of course, been appreciated beforehand. The enemy's defences were stronger than those encountered before and were in depth. The garrison had been alerted by the shooting at Alethangyaw; though the first bunker might possibly be surprised by stealth, the second could not. The unlikelihood of surprise was precisely Cartwright's reason for the mortars.

Mooring replied: 'Not much we can do before daylight, Watson, but I think we had better close up a bit before the moon.'

'I've been thinking about that, Satan, and I've got an idea. We might spring a surprise by making the Japs think we've tried to make a raid, as we've done before, but have got cold feet or couldn't find their positions and gone home again or that it's only a diversion from the Alethangyaw show.'

'How are we going to do that?'

'Set fire to a few huts.'

'I don't see the point of that.'

'Put yourself in their place. They see a few huts go up in flames, but nothing happens afterwards. They'll say it is just another little British tip-and-run raid. They'll think we've boobed and after a time they'll stand down.'

Mooring took a lot of convincing, but finally agreed. Holmes accordingly walked forward and set alight a few huts by the simple process of applying a match to the eaves of the thatched roofs. Dry as tinder, the thatch and bamboo burst instantly into vivid sheets of flame, crackling fiercely. They burned steadily for an hour or more, while all eyes were turned watchfully in the direction of the enemy bunkers.

The thinking had been right. The Japanese made no move. They were not going to risk another ambush, nor were they going to disclose their positions. The British would just go away if led to believe that there was no one there. The bashas did not matter a bit; let them burn.

When the flames had died down Mooring cautiously moved his men a little nearer to the enemy and, to intercept any possible enemy reinforcements, he sent a platoon under Lieutenant Bill Bond to cover a track to the south-east. Soon afterwards the huge full moon sailed up from above the hills behind them, brilliantly illuminating the scene with silver-blue light. Kanyindan was like a flood-lit stadium.

Another long wait followed, now pregnant with expectation. From somewhere not far off the heavy silence was shattered by the hoolock's blood-curdling laugh. No less alarming, because it sounded like stealthy human movement, an ant-eater scrabbled among the leaves beneath the kanyin trees. Occasional bursts of distant musketry and light machine-gun fire bore witness to the marines' battle at Alethangyaw. Holmes, inwardly trembling with excitement, admired the steady calm of Mooring, though he seemed a bit testy. He kept glancing at his watch and looking up at the sky. At long last the moon began to blanch and fade away as his conquering rival faintly heralded his approach beyond the hills.

Dawn disclosed sufficiently that the enemy position, as reported by V Force agents, consisted of two trench systems about eighty yards apart, the larger of which contained the gun. The smaller trench, manned by infantry, was only sixty yards away from the Africans; it was known to have some over-head cover and dug-out sleeping quarters. Mooring now, having sniffed the direction of the wind. broke wireless silence and spoke to Cartwright at Dodan, asking for Purdy's and Mitra's mortars to put down smoke on the enemy's nearer position.

Very soon afterwards battle was joined. The first mortar bomb was heard whispering in the air and a moment later, with uncanny accuracy, scored a direct hit on the trench.

A white, oily cloud of dense smoke billowed out lazily, followed rapidly by others, totally obscuring the scene. Under its cover the Africans closed in at the double, and, as the smoke thinned, tossed their grenades and jumped in with bayonets ready.

To their astonishment, the trench was empty and the Japanese were discernible at a distance, running hard for the main defences. The surprise, achieved in a new form, had been complete. To the Japanese, fresh from the Pacific, the sudden and mysterious eruption of choking smoke, possibly poisonous, right in their midst, arriving out of the blue in the apparent peacefulness of the dawn, must have been an unnerving and totally new experience.

The Africans, themselves coughing a little, promptly occupied the trench that they had won and faced the second one. This was going to be a far harder nut to crack. The opportunities for another surprise were few, though not exhausted. The Japanese were directly between Mooring on the east and Cartwright's mortars on the west. Southwards, on the Nigerians' left, the ground sloped away to the muddy Alethangyaw Chaung, now at low water, and beyond the chaung was a track that led to the village of that name.

The enemy opened fire briskly from his main position, obliging the Africans to keep their heads down. Reid Ross, the craggy Scot, returning to Mooring's command post with his orderly, Auta Kanem, had to go to ground and crawl back to the cover of the village. The Japanese position was so well concealed that for a long time it could not be identified and the Africans could not return fire until, eventually, a little movement was spotted on the face of a large bund. The Troop leaders then realized that this bund constituted the defensive rear of the enemy position and that his marksmen were shooting through camouflaged slits scooped out of it.

Thereupon the Africans began, in Ross's words, 'to return fire into these slits, single shots, very effectively'. The enemy's fire soon slackened and Mooring decided that this was the moment to assault. He called for high explosives from the mortars and very quickly the bombs were flighting down to burst fairly accurately on their target. He then ordered Burgess's troop to close in.

Fortunately there was a little shallow chaung that gave Burgess a covered approach for part of the way. Mooring and Holmes watched the Troop crawling closer and closer and the mortar fire was called off. At a range of a cricket pitch a grenade battle began. Burgess at once began to sustain casualties and he himself was severely wounded.

The frontal attack having failed, the momentum of the attack was maintained by classic little manœuvres on either flank. On the left, Ross, taking with him Sergeant Ali Yola and Musa Congo, carrying a Bren-gun and extra magazines, slipped down into the dead ground, crossed the Alethangyaw Chaung and worked their way round till they had a good view of the rear of the enemy's bund position. From there they opened fire, doing such great execution that the Japanese went to ground and 'appeared to have had it'.

The three then began to make their way back to the squadron when, to their surprise, they saw Holmes, in one of his moods of impetuosity, running out to meet them. He did not hear, or chose to ignore, Mooring's cry of: 'Don't be a bloody fool; come back!'

He had seen a few Japs breaking away and, as he came up to Ross on the bank of the chaung, he called out:

'Quick, Reid; your Bren!'

Then, seeing that the ground was wet and difficult for a Bren-gun, he added:

'Here, I'll give you a back.'

He went down on all fours and the subaltern, using him as a rest for his gun, quickly picked off two of the enemy, while Musa, dropping on one knee, picked off a third with his rifle.

Meantime a similar little manœuvre was carried out on the right flank, where Mooring ordered Sergeant Hugh Elder to take out a section and attack the enemy from that side also. The sergeant executed his little operation with great skill, giving a text-book demonstration of the manœuvre of 'fire and move-ment', making good use of the bunds of the paddy-fields. At one point two Japanese jumped up from behind a bund and threw two grenades. They failed to explode and the Japs instantly disappeared behind the bunds. A little farther on he encountered four more Japs in a kneeling position that seemed to imply surrender, but Elder had been well instructed in Japanese surrender tricks and took no chances. Three were shot or bayoneted forthwith and the fourth – a big husky fellow – was seized and made prisoner, 'just to show', as he said afterwards, 'that we can take 'em alive sometimes'.

Mooring now closed in on the enemy with both Troops, Burgess's being now led by Sergeant Houston. To everyone's great surprise, the Japanese resistance suddenly collapsed. Direct hits from the mortars had cut them up severely. Caught between these from one direction, the attacking infantry on another and seeing Elder's section coming in from a third, they thought, no doubt, that the game was up. There remained only a few of them in the gun pit and these were swiftly dispatched by a volley of grenades, immediately followed up by the machete and bayonet. Holmes himself killed two. The victorious Africans swarmed over the enemy position, their gleaming white teeth set in jubilant smiles in the bright morning sun, their weapons stained with the blood of their enemies. Twenty-seven

Japanese lay dead around them, for the loss of only three of their comrades. Such as were left of the garrison bolted. Some ran to Dodan, where they were brusquely halted by the Bren-guns at the Africans' mortar position. They turned and joined a crowd of other fleeing Japanese in the dead ground of the Alethangyaw Chaung where they met a murderous fire from the marines. The enemy artillery officer, bleeding from huge gashes by machetes, was still alive, defiant and haughty, refusing medical aid; he was allowed his wish and departed to his an-cestors some hours later.

In due time the gun was manhandled away, for dispatch to Maungdaw, together with the prisoner. It was the second gun that the Africans had captured, a record in which any regiment might have taken pride.

The next day the Africans and the commandos learnt with delight that both Razabil and Buthidaung had fallen to 5th and 7th Divisions, but Holmes heard with regret a day or two later that 'Digger' Morrison, commanding the 1st Battalion of his own regiment, had been killed. There was still much hard fighting to be done up in those jungle hills.

The Africans continued to hold Kanyindan and the Lamba-guna bridge until relieved by 5th Commando five nights later, by which time Oliver Hunt had succeeded Mooring. At Kanyindan they dug in well at a new position, thinly protected by a little wire left by the Japanese. The Japanese mortared them from time to time and made one of their stupid jitter raids. They cock-crowed, barked like dogs and called out: 'Hello Johnnie; this is Nippon soldier.' They hoped either to frighten the Africans or else to force them to disclose their positions. The Africans treated them with contempt and withheld their fire.

For Holmes there followed a period of intense activity as 'Screwdriver' continued to twist home, at times uncertainly, encountering knots. Basing himself first on the Africans' trenches, he went here, there and everywhere, serving as Intelligence officer to each of the Screwdriver units in turn. Except for the mortaring that he had to sit through at Kanyin-dan, he relished it all. The gleam of magic in the air had never been so bright. On the very day after the battle had opened he sneaked into Alethangyaw, which was not occupied by the

Marines, and had another meeting with Rob Roy, who was lying low at a secret place that he knew of.

Dewdrop Inn at Ginger Creek was mortared and machine-gunned one day but its landlord was never there and for eleven days and nights he shared the trenches of the Tarantulas and the commandos.

The Marines Drive Inland

While the West Africans were marching southwards to attack Kanyindan on the night of 11 March, 44th Royal Marine Commando, together with Nonweiler's advanced headquarters, was sailing across the bay from the romantic shores of Coconut Island in fourteen 'Landing Craft Personnel' and one 'Head-quarters Ship' of the Royal Indian Navy in two waves. Above them hung a brilliant canopy of stars; below and all around them flashes of phosphorescence sparkled on the surface of the Bay of Bengal.

After four and a half years of training without firing a shot at the enemy, all were mad-keen for action, each man with his private feelings swallowed up in the corporate comradeship of a well-knit unit. Horton had unfolded the plot to everyone ashore: they knew that they would have to locate the enemy positions in the dark, without reconnaissance, and attack them at close quarters with grenade and bayonet, without the help of artillery. It was going to be man versus man. All officers (as did those of 5th Commando) carried rifles. The 'Marx Brothers', including the shaggy Harpo and Osiullah, were with them and so were a few uniformed men of the Burma Intelligence Corps under Lieutenant Tom Tin. Also with the marines were two men of the 55th Observation Squadron, whose task, as it had been to the Africans on a previous occasion, was to deceive the enemy with simulated battle noises whenever required.

As we have seen earlier, the town of Alethangyaw, long and straggling, lay a little inland and parallel to the coast. The Japs had one small post in a group of fishermen's huts close to the shore, but their main position was sited towards the eastern end of the town and incorporated some of the civilians' air-raid shelters, which had been converted into bunkers. Most formidable of them promised to be a bunker built beneath a bungalow, like the one beside the tennis court of heroic memory at Kohima.

A thousand yards to westward of the main village, astride the main road from the north, there was also a small cluster of trenches and weapon pits. We shall refer to these as the West and the East positions. From V Force information it was known that the two garrisons numbered probably about eighty or more men, with machine-guns but no artillery. The Kanyindan position lay nearly two miles farther to the west. Nonweiler's orders to Horton were to overcome the Japanese in Alethangyaw and then to penetrate to a point in the hills some five miles inland and from there to dominate the coastal strip. They were to carry four days' rations.

After the marines had been on passage from Coconut Island for about an hour, the Arakan coast began to resolve itself as a dark smudge of charcoal on the horizon, silent, without lights, mysterious and hostile. As they closed the shore, the hands manning the landing craft became very nervous and it was only with difficulty that they were urged to close within landing distance. Even so, the crew of one craft, when they saw the phosphorescent waves breaking on the gleaming white beach, lost their heads and let go their kedge anchor so far out that one of the commando sections, led by Lieutenant Philip Rider, was precipitated into deep water and several of them totally immersed.

But by 11.30, which was the prescribed time for the first of the waves, a good landing had been made at a point where a track came down to the beach. There was no opposition. A Troop (Captain Baxter) and D Troop (Captain Winter) formed the first wave and twenty minutes later Horton followed with his headquarters and three more troops, with the last of the six troops on their heels. In the high surf everybody got very wet.

Baxter's and Winter's troops made at once for the main enemy East position, the one being directed to approach it from the left, the other from the right, in a 'pincer movement'. They were soon in trouble. Horton quickly established a temporary headquarters a few hundred yards from the shore, where he expected to meet representatives from Baxter and Winter with situation reports. None arrived, so, followed by Captain Martin's C Troop, he pushed forward to the locality of the enemy's West position, where he found that B Troop, under Captain Edward Sturges, had successfully assaulted a small enemy machine-gun post and killed the occupants. Sturges, however was under desultory rifle fire, some of which came from Japanese snipers hidden in trees and it was not until nearly daylight that they were located and dealt with by one of the troop's own snipers, Marine Deacon.

Horton became anxious about A and D Troops in their attempt against the main enemy position to the east. Listening to their wireless signals, it seemed evident that they had been unable to identify the Japanese position and were in a state of some confusion, experiencing all the difficulties of fighting at night in the heart of a town. He therefore resolved to go and see for himself.

Turning right, he made for the main town and on entering the market-place came under fire from well-concealed snipers in trees and behind buildings. He noticed with professional interest that the Japs allowed his small party to pass before opening fire on them from behind. Pushing on, he was able to find Baxter's troop in possession of some Japanese weapon pits on the western side of the market-place, but pinned down by fire from unseen snipers in trees and from light machine-guns which were impossible to locate in the darkness. Surprise had not been effected.

Horton knew that this was the area, forming a shallow depression, in which the Japanese had built their strongest positions and he supposed that they had voluntarily abandoned some of them in favour of ambush tactics. He was struck by the fact that the enemy fire was very erratic and haphazard and, like all night shooting by inferior marksmen, was going high, and he quickly assessed that the fire, though highly disconcerting, was not dangerous.

More discomforting to Horton was the fact that he could not discover the situation of D Troop with any certainty, though he could talk to Winter by radio. He realized then that it had been a mistake to order the two troops to make a 'pincer' attack by separate approaches and that they should have been launched together in one combined attack. He therefore, by radio, ordered Winter to take his Troop round to the north of the town and Captain Martin to bring C Troop from the West position, pass through A Troop and drive straight through the town. This was a contingency for which he had provided in the original plan.

Twenty minutes passed without any sign of C Troop. Horton therefore turned back westward again and visited Martin. He found that his Troop was under fire from the front and that one of its sections was missing. He ordered Martin to move at once and rejoined his own command post, where his second-in-command, Major John Macafee, was so severely concussed by a violent blow on the head from his own rifle, which had been struck by an enemy bullet, that he had to be evacuated; this was the first of several casualties in Horton's headquarters.

More unsatisfactory news continued to flow in on the air. From Winter he learnt that a section of D Troop under Lieutenant Gus White was missing, and from Martin he heard that C Troop, having moved a few hundred yards eastwards into Alethangyaw, had become pinned down by enemy snipers.

In fact, White's section of D Troop had had a stiff little fight. Having successfully cleared part of the town, they had reached the fortified bungalow which appeared to be the enemy's main strongpoint. Here, after White had sent off a report to Horton, the remainder came under fire from the bunker under the bungalow and from other weapon pits, but White went for it without hesitation. Using the text-book method, he and four other men attacked from one quarter while the remainder, under Sergeant MacKenzie, moved to a flank to give fire support with automatics. To their consternation, all the automatic weapons jammed, having been immersed in the sea when the men had been put down into deep water from the landing craft. White's little party therefore had to attack without fire support. He himself was painfully wounded and Corporal Bedford killed. Unable to locate the enemy weapons satisfactorily in the dark and continuing to be under severe fire, White withdrew his men and led them out to the north.

His attempts to make contact with the rest of D Troop being

unsuccessful, White advanced independently up into the hills, since that was the Commando's objective, picking up a few strays and arriving at 3.30 in the morning. His map having been shot to pieces in his pocket when he had been hit, he had very little to guide him and was extremely lucky to by-pass the enemy detachments scattered about the plain. Himself in great pain, he found Sergeant MacKenzie a grand leader and an inspiration to all the young marines in their dangerous and nerve-testing experiences.

Having gone a good deal too far west, White could not find the rest of the commando during the following day, so, gallantly supported by MacKenzie, he led his men down again from the hills to make contact with the West Africans at the Lambaguna bridge.

He reached the bridge in pitch darkness and was faced with the problem of how to gain admission past the Sierra Leonians, for he knew their reputation for literal obedience to orders and that they had been told to 'shoot on sight and no questions'. A little mother-wit served him well, however. Having got his men safely down behind a paddy-bund, he walked forward alone, shouting all the foul language he could think of. He reckoned that they would be startled and would hold fire. They did.

Of all this Horton knew nothing until the battle was over. By the time that he had learnt of the unsatisfactory situation in Alethangyaw it was 4 o'clock in the morning, with a brilliant moon riding the sky above the Mayu hills. Evidently it was now impossible for the commando to reach its objective in the hills before daylight. Regretfully Horton decided that he must concentrate his force and resume his objective on the next night. Nonweiler, who was offshore in the Headquarters Ship, gave approval by radio.

The concentration was effected with little interference from the enemy in a group of compounds near the West position. Defences were immediately dug and the Army medical officer, Captain C. A. McCleary, came forward to establish an Aid Post, where, faithful to tradition, the commando's naval chaplain, the Rev. H. C. W. Manger, joined him. From first light onwards the position was subjected to almost continuous fire from snipers and light machine-guns, but the Japanese made no attempt to attack.

Soon after daybreak Cartwright's mortaring of Kanyindan could be plainly seen and heard away to the left. Shortly afterwards, in the early morning sunlight, the astonished eyes of Sturges's troop, who were on the extreme left, saw a drove of Japanese, to the number of at least 150, running hell-for-leather straight towards them from Kanyindan, obviously making for what they believed to be the safety of Alethangyaw.

B Troop and most of X Troop, with Horton himself as spectator, had a spectacular field day, shooting down nearly all of them, many of whom were killed by Corporal Parkinson's skilful use of his 2-inch mortar, the base plate of which he held at an angle of 45°, the heel only on the ground. For many days afterwards Denis Holmes, who was constantly to-and-fro in these parts, could see the bloated corpses ebbing and flowing with the tides in the Alethangyaw Chaung.

Horton had now to make a fresh plan for resuming on the second night his advance north-eastwards across the coastal plain and up into the hills, where his designated objective was the elongated Hill 250. He could now make a visual appreciation of the situation. Beyond the flat and open paddy-fields to the north-east, he saw the abrupt eruption of the jungle-clad foothills, which had the appearance of a solid green wall, the features in which were extremely difficult to identify. The map showed a tightly packed mass of wriggly contour lines, cleft here and there with chaungs.

On his right front, however, a chaung, known as the Taungbo, meandered across the plain in a serpentine course from Alethangyaw to a point in the hills. He had duly noted this in his preliminary thinking and had decided to take this point as a guide, march to it on an exact compass bearing, and then to follow a wriggly line of lesser chaungs which led to his objective.

To do this he would have to cross the Taungbo Chaung at some point and he ordered Captain Oliver Hamlin, of X Troop, to send out a patrol to discover whether the chaung was fordable. Hamlin sent out Second-Lieutenant Alister Mac-Kinnon, but, after making good progress for about a mile and a half, the patrol came under fire. MacKinnon was mortally wounded and Marine Kennedy apparently killed. The Japanese, in the manner that they had, dragged Kennedy out in the open paddy and covered his body by fire to prevent rescue, but it was recovered that night by friends of V Force.

All through the 12th the heat in the compounds was stifling and the flies multitudinous and it was with difficulty that the sweating marines, in action for the first time, learned their first lesson in snatching a little sleep in the crackle of musketry. Having evacuated his wounded through the safe corridor of the West Africans at Kanyindan, Horton gave his orders verbally to his troop commanders for the next night. He knew by now, from interjections obviously coming from the enemy, that they had netted on his radio and, having sent a rude message to the Japs, he therefore followed his verbal orders with bogus ones on the radio and established a code with his troop commanders by which they would know in future when his orders were bogus or genuine.

He had scarcely finished these arrangements when, at about half past five, all his three positions came under fire from artillery and heavy mortars from Point 211 in the hills, which was to become a thorn in the sides of both commandos. In the absence of any supporting artillery of his own, there was nothing that Horton could do about it, but fortunately there was only about another hour of daylight and at 7.30, as the mosquitoes swarmed in the dark and the bats fluttered and wheeled around the bashas, the commando moved out north-east for the hills, led by X Troop under Hamlin, making a bee-line by compass to the point ordered by Horton.

The night was black as pitch and from time to time the marines clung to the bayonet scabbards of the men in front to maintain contact. The little party from the Observation Squadron went with them but left their apparatus behind in the vacated positions to go on making deceptive noises till midnight.

At first all went well. By good fortune they avoided the pockets of enemy troops that they had expected to encounter. They forded the Taungbo satisfactorily, though the water was up to the necks of the shorter men. Difficulties began, however, at the point on the edge of the hills where Horton had ordered a halt. Some of the troops were found to be mixed up and several sections were missing altogether. They were entering the jungle now and all the mysterious noises of jungle night life were around them. After a short pause to reorganize, the advance into the hills continued.

They had left the Taungbo Chaung and were now following a tributary that twisted about among the jungle-clad hills, with one or two deceptive sub-tributaries. As noiselessly as possible, the marines clambered forward, desperately slowly, as the vegetation became thicker and thicker, the hills steeper and steeper. The whispering bamboos, dense as a Greek phalanx and much taller, obscured vision and baffled hearing.

About 2 a.m. the huge moon topped the crest of the Mayu hills, its light playing queer tricks among the trees, so that men saw strange moving shapes about them. Its brilliance was startling and Horton had to decide that it would be impossible to gain Hill 250 before daylight and that there must be yet another night halt, though in a position that was far from secure.

Leaving a detachment at the chaung junction to gather in any of the lost sheep, he formed a defensive box in some elevated ground near by. Everyone was very wet, but there was no shooting that night and the crackles of musketry and grenades were replaced by the demented cackles of the hoolock monkey, the eldritch howls of jackal and hyaenas and the restless scrabblings, squeaks and grunts of jungle life, while the myriad frogs blurted out their harsh chorus in the chaungs below.

Daylight revealed the position to be a scrubby, flat area, overlooked by hills on several sides. Horton accordingly posted picquets on the adjacent high ground and sent out several patrols.[1] One of these, led by Hamlin, made its way successfully to Hill 250 and found it totally unsuitable for its intended purpose. Another patrol, under Sturges, clambered up a dominant hill and was rewarded by a fine, commanding view of the plain below with parties of Japanese moving about, many of whom fell to the marksmanship of Marine N. R. Gurd, another of B Troop's snipers. Watched by the approving eye of Sergeant Webber, he dropped them one after another at long range.

A third patrol, under Rider, made a longer penetration

---

[1] 'When in a doubtful situation, choose a firm base, concentrate your forces and reconnoitre widely' – Field-Marshal Montgomery.

southwards to the lofty Point 346 overlooking the road that ran along the foothills (as 5 Commando was also to find) and inflicted many casualties on the enemy without loss to themselves.

Some of the stragglers came in during the forenoon and Horton learnt by radio that most of the others, of whom Baxter had taken command, had gathered on another hill-top, from which they had excellent observation on the road over which the commando had been ordered to exercise surveillance and on the enemy gun and mortar positions at Point 211 which had bothered them the previous evening. Horton ordered them to stay there and report all enemy activities.

It was not long, however, before the commando's main position on its little plateau was spotted by the enemy, who kept it under desultory fire most of the day, scattering the startled monkeys. Horton's command post suffered most. Simultaneously, and as though by the same bullet, he, his adjutant (Captain Peter Parish) and the chaplain were all hit. Parish escaped with a slight wound in the face. Horton was hit close to the eye and knocked out but, after having had the wound dressed by McCleary and having had a short rest, was able to carry on. The chaplain's wound, however, was mortal.

All through that day the marines sat watchfully on their hill-tops under a vehement sun, seeking the shade and getting such sleep as could fitfully be snatched. Unable to light any fires, they had nothing to eat throughout the operation but cold rations from their packs and chlorinated water. Along the chaungs below them the snipe and kingfishers wheeled and flashed, with the expectant vultures ever overhead.

Before dark Horton called in his patrols and at about 7.45, to the rasping croak of the nightjar, the commando began its third night's operations. In view of Hamlin's report on Point 250, Horton had during the day picked out an obviously better position about 1,000 yards north of where he now was. Proceeding again along the line of a chaung, the commando took over four hours to get there, through very wet, dense and difficult country and in Stygian darkness, but a satisfactory box was established soon after midnight and it could be said at last that the designated objective had been gained. Here it might be possible for the commando to carry out its allotted mission for a short time.

Men were beginning to drag their feet now but at daylight on 14 April offensive patrols began again, in pursuit of the tactical purpose of the expedition. Hamlin laid an ambush on a known enemy track but no victims appeared. Sturges, on the other hand, went out due south to the high Point 346, became engaged in a series of spirited engagements which lasted until late afternoon in sweltering heat and in which casualties were inflicted on the enemy.

Horton was expecting to be relieved by 5th Commando on the night of 14 March, but late in the day he learnt from Nonweiler by radio that he was to withdraw without being relieved. A withdrawal through enemy territory in such circumstances was an extremely tricky business, so 44 Commando was to have yet a fourth night of operations. Horton, having arranged for the deceivers of the Observation Squadron to leave behind their contraptions for making more misleading noises, ordered withdrawal to begin soon after dark to a concentration area at a chaung junction. The movement was made successfully, but the mixed elements under Baxter, had a running fight with a party of the enemy. Another enemy party made a vain onslaught, with their usual war-whoops, against Baxter's box as soon as he had left it.

Having concentrated, the commando began to move down towards the plain after moonrise at about one o'clock, with Hamlin's X Troop again leading. All were now very tired. As they approached the plain in the revealing moonlight some of the troops came under fire first from light machine-guns and soon afterwards from grenades. There was a great deal of very disconcerting noise which gave the impression of an ambush in force, but most of the fire was ill-directed, flying high. The commando were momentarily disconcerted but shook it off, incurring five casualties, and eventually, after a very trying march of some six miles, made good their withdrawal through the West Africans' securely held box at Kanyindan.

Horton felt very nervous that the Nigerians would mistake them in the moonlight for the enemy and open fire, but Mooring's men behaved with perfect propriety and, after the proper challenge, the tired green berets marched through 'all those black faces' in good order, having suffered only twenty-one casualties in an operation in which, by aggressive pursuit of their purpose, by courage shown on many occasions, by physical fitness and by Horton's very good and level-headed leadership, they had reached the territorial objective against which they had been sent, had rattled the enemy and inflicted casualties. Tactically, 'Screwdriver' had only partly fulfilled its purpose, but that was soon to be put right.

5th Commando Sees Them Off

As the marines pulled out from their bridgehead, 5th Commando, accompanied by their attachments from V Force and from the Burma Intelligence Corps, were sailing in to replace them. They were to operate in rather a different manner and to provoke sharp reactions from the enemy.

David Shaw, their CO, was a blend of many fine qualities. He believed strongly in the Christian religion and the good life, yet was full of fun and gaiety. The scar that he bore on his forehead from the claws of a leopard testified that he was acquainted with danger and his jutting jaw symbolized an aggressive spirit. In tactics his reactions were quick and his methods forthright rather than subtle.

In accordance with Nonweiler's orders, Shaw landed his commando not as the marines had done but from river craft on the muddy banks of the big chaung flowing out north of No-Can-Do known as the Ton, where he was met by the ubiquitous and cheerful Holmes. From there he marched to the white sand dunes south of Alethangyaw and began to dig a defensive base near the beach, where the Royal Indian Navy was expected to land his supplies and evacuate his casualties. The place was, however, very exposed to observation on the landward side, as was very soon to be demonstrated.

While the defences were being dug and Captain Walker, the doctor, was setting up his first-aid post, Shaw himself led two troops straight into the slumbrous heat of Alethangyaw, where he met Holmes again, together with Rob Roy. There were no Japanese in the village and at nightfall Shaw withdrew to his base, which the Japanese 75-mm gun at Point 211 had already spotted and was shelling in a spasmodic fashion.

The aggressive Shaw promptly sent out Captain Richard Sheddon's No. 4 Troop to find and destroy the enemy position. Sheddon (who had won the Military Cross in Madagascar) was out all night, but his task was a pretty hopeless one, as the only guidance he had was a compass bearing on the gun somewhere in the thick hill-jungle. All they found was a recently vacated position of some sort, with fresh mule droppings.

An hour or so before dawn on the next morning (the 15th) Shaw, rightly feeling sensitive about Alethangyaw, told Captain 'Chips' Heron, small, tubby and jolly, to take 3 Troop into the village. Heron and his men, new to the country, found the experience an eerie one. The moonlight played confusingly upon the thick bamboo groves that fringed the town and their tall stems made loud reports as the men clawed their way through. The town dogs added to the racket but Heron found the place still free of the enemy. Throughout these operations and for some time afterwards the situation in Alethangyaw was nearly always uncertain. It was never permanently garrisoned by the British forces, for it harboured enemy agents as well as friendly ones and was considered a 'security risk'. Occasionally the enemy made quick incursions into it, but did not stay long.

As the sun rose on the morning of the 15th it smote down with all the savagery of its pre-monsoon ill temper, its heat supplemented by the spasmodic fire from the hateful Point 211. The commandos sweated as they dug deep in the white sand. It was a day of intense activity as Shaw sent out his offensive patrols far and wide.

At 10 o'clock he gave Captain Kerr, leader of 5 Troop, the special mission of making for Point 346, that eminence on the edge of the hill-jungle where the marines had had good play against the enemy. Any troops might well have blanched at such an assignment. Two and a half miles of flat, naked country, dominated by the far hills, had to be traversed in the strong light of a tropic sun. None the less, 5 Troop formed up and advanced with battle-drill precision in open formation across the bare, uncompromising paddy. The field-gun and the heavy mortars from Point 211 soon gave voice to their malevolence and men began to drop. The rate of fire became heavy but 5 Troop never wavered and they won Point 346 at a cost of two killed and fourteen wounded. At last light they returned to the box, carrying their wounded.

Meanwhile Shaw had reconnoitred for another concentration area, but got shelled there also. He determined therefore that something serious would have to be done about the infernal Point 211. He had asked for an air strike against it, but had been refused. So that night he set out against it himself with 2 and 5 Troops, the latter leading, and the whole force moving in single file so that men could walk on the raised paddy-bunds without having to clamber over them repeatedly. Osiullah accompanied them. The night was very dark and for the first thousand yards nothing broke the stillness but the harsh squawk of the nightjar.

At that point they clashed suddenly with a large Japanese column which, it was learned later, was 100 strong and had been intended to attack the commando's box. They came in on the column's right. Their approach was clearly heard, for, in typical Japanese fashion, they were chattering noisily, with clink of accoutrements. The commandos turned immediately and engaged them at very close quarters. The main clash occurred about midway in the column, where the head of 5 Troop, led by Shaw's adjutant, Captain Eric Holt, joined Shaw's headquarters party at the tail of 5 Troop. There was a fierce and deadly gun-fight in the dark with automatics, grenades and rifles, the black void stabbed with rifle flashes, with streams of coloured tracer and with the orange bursts of grenades.

Holt ordered 2 Troop to fix bayonets, but contact was never close enough for their use. Instead, there was a wild fire-fight of considerable intensity, very chancy, difficult to control and a severe test of nerves and training. Every fifth man was killed or wounded, but the commandos stood their ground and it was the Japanese who were seen off. They fell back suddenly and the night was seized by an uneasy silence.

Shaw, determined to pursue his objective, resumed his advance with 5 Troop and ordered Holt to take the other back to the defensive box, together with some of the casualties. There

Holt ordered a very tight stand-to. The Japanese closed in on them to within a few yards, but the commandos' discipline was such that they withheld their fire, lay dead quiet, and did not disclose their positions. At about 4 a.m. the enemy stole away, leaving twenty dead to be counted by V Force. From later reports it was evident that the Japanese brigade commander, alarmed by the marines' successful landing and by the persistent presence of British troops in the area, had sent in reinforcements to drive the invaders out.

At first light on the 16th Holt sent out a patrol with stretcher parties to bring in the rest of the night's casualties. Their total was found to be ten killed and ten wounded. The gallant scout Osiullah had also been killed. The casualties had to be evacuated by sea and Holt ordered Lieutenant Ray Noble to lead a patrol down to the beach with the doctor. They moved in wide arrow-head formation, but the gun from Point 211 was on to them. Two men were killed by shell-fire, Sergeant Dalziel badly wounded and Noble blown to the ground by blast. At the beach the surf was found to be running ten feet high. The stretcher-bearers and the unfortunate wounded were swamped over and over again and, as the landing-craft had no ramps, the stretchers had to be lifted over the gunwales.

At 8 o'clock on the morning of the 16th Holt learnt from Shaw on the radio that he and 5 Troop were at Point 346, having himself been unable to locate 211. He told Holt that he intended to stay there, as from Point 346 he could dominate the plain below and observe the enemy gun position. Holt soon formed the impression that the plain had now been cleared of enemy, for Lieutenant Gordon Dashwood, taking a ration party up to Point 346 met no Japs (though it took him six hours to get there and back) and an all-night patrol by Sheddon's Troop found Alethangyaw still clear also. To this extent, therefore, the mission had been fulfilled.

The impression was strengthened when, at last light, 5 Troop reported from Point 346 that a party of eighty Japs, with mules and carrying casualties, was withdrawing to the south along the road that skirted the hills. No doubt this was the residue of the column that had attacked Shaw the night before. A splendid target for guns and aircraft, but none was on call.

Throughout that day the box had been shelled intermittently, but otherwise that was virtually the end of the scrapping. Fresh orders arrived from Nonweiler to meet a new situation. They informed Shaw that, according to V Force intelligence, the enemy intended to cut his line of communications, that the navy could no longer supply him or evacuate his casualties over the Alethangyaw beach and that he was to take over the positions held by the West Africans, who would be leaving the area in two days' time.

Accordingly, Shaw was now to move down from the hills, vacate his box on the Alethangyaw beach, establish a new base in the locality that we have called Alethangyaw West, deploy his troops in the villages of the plain and continue offensive patrolling. Further orders told him to make contact on the north with the 2nd West Yorkshires and to maintain close contact with Holmes.

The withdrawals from the hills and from the Alethangyaw base were accomplished with great difficulty and lasted all the night of 17/18 March. Shaw established his headquarters at Dodan, while Sheddon stood rearguard at Alethangyaw West and patrols went out into the main village and up into the hills.

On the evening of the 20th Sheddon's rearguard was withdrawn, except for a covering section under Ray Noble. Here he was visited at last light by Rob Roy, who had stolen out from Alethangyaw at great risk to warn him that 'a Japanese force of many men' was approaching. This without doubt was the force, or part of it, that V Force had reported. Noble and his men, with the big Alethangyaw Chaung in full flood behind them, passed an anxious night and next morning, before getting permission to withdraw (by swimming), they saw the Japanese re-entering Alethangyaw.

Meanwhile some artillery support had at last been provided and Captain Graham, of 6th Medium Regiment, Royal Artillery, arrived to shell the infernal Point 211 with a 5·5-inch gun. Holmes had been tickled when his scouts had informed him that it was the lair of Lieutenant Honu and was accordingly called Honu-ghati by the Chittagonians. Very difficult to identify in the thick hill-jungle, it was picked out for the gunner observation officer by a V Force scout. After a few ranging rounds at extreme range, accurate 'fire for effect' was brought down, to the delight of the scout, who exclaimed: 'Allah be praised! May that be the end of Lieutenant Honu.' The next day the RAF joined in and bombed the hill from Hurricanes. Unfortunately, after Noble's section had been withdrawn, Alethangyaw was also bombed. Holmes was himself at No-Can-Do that day and it was with bitter feelings that he watched the aircraft scream down over his head, his only comfort being that he had warned his friends there in time.

Late that same day, which was 21 March, 5th Commando was in its turn relieved by the marines and left for Maungdaw for what they hoped would be a rest. They had had a full week of strenuous operations by day and night and had lost fourteen men killed and twenty-nine wounded, but they had adequately fulfilled their mission of dominating the plain, Holmes having reported it to be clear of enemy when he called to say good-bye. The men now looked forward to some decent, body-filling food after the concentrated vitamins on which they had subsisted. They also looked forward to a shave; it had been a mistake to send them in without razors, for a shaggy chin does no good to a soldier's 'morale'.

Before 5th Commando pulled out Denis Holmes had had the sad duty of saying good-bye to the cheerful Black Tarantulas. They were to pass over the hills to rejoin their own division and assume a surveillance mission on 15th Corps' left flank. At the same time Cartwright was promoted to command the 6th West African Brigade, being succeeded by Bernard Shattock, with Mooring as second-in-command. Holmes, who had been out on patrol the night before, saw them off at No-Can-Do on 17 March. To both the Africans and to the V Force the break-up of the partnership was a wrench. Even the giant Yaro, as he trudged off behind Satan Mooring, no longer wore his habitual grin.

The Tarantulas had played an effective and significant part in operations, which has never received the recognition that it deserves. They had operated in a commando role with conspicuous success. They had inflicted appreciable losses on the enemy out of all proportion to the numbers employed. They had captured two Japanese field-guns and two prisoners and had made valuable identifications. They had opened the way to the seizure of territory some twelve miles long by three miles wide. They had obliged the enemy to lock up a substantial force for the protection of his flank instead of being thrown into the main battle. In all, they had made 150 patrols and raids.

The Africans, in their turn, would have been quite in the dark without the accurate information of V Force, the skilful and daring guidance of its scouts and the audacious example of its leader. Bernard Shattock wrote of him:

'Holmes was a remarkable man, immensely respected by Europeans and Africans alike. Always full of purpose, positive and vigorously aggressive. Always scheming, always planning, always determined to procure the right information so vital for success. Without him life would have been difficult on the Arakan coast for the Tarantulas.'

Another sad duty for Holmes had been to see Osiullah's father. The old man had taken his son's death with fortitude and dignity. He gently declined Holmes's offer of compensation, shaking his head slowly and saying:

'It is the will of Allah, sahib. May He bring the British a speedy victory.'

With these simple words the old man salaamed and left. His spirit was typical of the stoical resistance of the loyal villagers in Burma. The British and Indian soldiers, moving from one battle front to another, rarely appreciated how agonizing were the problems facing the villagers, especially those of Muslim faith. They had seen the British successfully occupying nearly the whole of the peninsula the year before, had watched their retreat and the return of the Japanese and now were again witnessing a surge forward by the British.

How long would the British stay this time? It seemed to them that the campaign was like the tides of the sea, ever flowing and ebbing. Their means of livelihood in the land were lost or imperilled, their villages burnt or evacuated. To which side should they pin their faith? The natural inclination of the Muslims in particular to look to the British as their protectors was sorely tried. The Japanese were merciless, the Mughs often vindictive and treacherous. Yet it was the humblest people, for the greater part, who remained steadfast.

Two days after the departure of the Tarantulas Holmes abandoned the Dewdrop Inn at Ginger Creek, which had proved inconvenient, and moved to a much better place at Nurullapara ('The Village of the Light of God'), where he was very comfortably installed in a schoolhouse which had its own water supply in the compound. He did not yet inhabit it himself, however, preferring to be out with the commandos. In his absence he brought the Sikh, 'Martin' Luthera, over from Teknaf to run its daily business of interrogation and administration. Japanese patrols were prowling about within sight and Khyber Khan had a good shoot with the Bren-gun.

Saving the Guns

Fifth Commando had been at Maungdaw for only one day when it was called upon to meet a totally unexpected emergency. The stirring little exploit that resulted, so long left in obscurity, had nothing to do with 'Screwdriver' but cannot be allowed to go unrecorded.

News arrived that a forward battery of mountain artillery on the edge of the foot-hills three miles away had been pinned down by infiltrating Japanese and was in grave danger of being overwhelmed. The commando was suddenly called upon to go to their assistance and Shaw at once sent out his second-in-command, Major Robin Stuart (himself a gunner), with 4 and 5 Troops under Richard Sheddon and Bill Kerr, to rescue them.

Shaw told them that this was a good opportunity to have a real crack at the Japs and all ranks responded to the occasion with a relish that would have excited the admiration of an Alexander or a Caesar. The morale was heaven-high and the troops sang all the way on the approach march until their officers had to stop them and order silence.

Stuart ordered Kerr's 5 Troop to make the attack, with 4 Troop in reserve in a defensive position close to the battery of 3·7-inch mountain howitzers. The terrain ahead was rough and broken jungle with a group of three steep hills predominating, very difficult for manœuvre, fire control and observation, but ideal for ambush, with here and there a flat paddy-field in the valleys.

The exact enemy locations were not known. The day had already well advanced into afternoon and there was no time for a carefully planned stratagem of text-book nicety. Stuart, after a quick appreciation, gave the simplest orders and Kerr's Troop went straight over the rough ground with tremendous gusto and in exemplary order. The Japanese, concealed among the trees, let them approach closely and then let fly with automatics, mortars and rifles. The Troop immediately took sharp casualties, but the remainder ignored the shock and pressed on in a high fighting spirit, the junior leaders inspired with initiative, every man responding instinctively to the call of the moment. A furious and confused fire-fight at close quarters went on until nearly dusk, but one by one the enemy posts were overcome or driven back half a mile or so. Two machine-guns were captured. Heavy casualties were inflicted.

Meanwhile, back at the battery position, 4 Troop listened with impatient expectancy to the shooting ahead and stood ready to go forward to support their comrades. The wireless sets failed to overcome the obstacles of the hills and no news came through of the fortunes of 5 Troop. Stuart sent out two officer patrols under Gordon Dashwood and Ken Waggett, but they made no contact. The sun declined and 4 Troop waited.

Late in the afternoon, with only another hour of daylight left, Troop-Sergeant-Major Foster, of 5 Troop, appeared out of the bush and asked for help in rescuing the wounded. Sheddon sent out Ray Noble with one subsection and a medical orderly, Lance-Corporal Walker.

Guided by Foster, who had taken a circuitous route to avoid observation, Noble hurried forward as best he could through the hilly jungle. After about a mile the jungle ended suddenly and beyond it lay a large stretch of open paddy. In the centre of this lay a cluster of 5 Troop's dead and wounded.

As soon as Noble's party emerged from the bush they were met by a hail of machine-gun and mortar fire. It was difficult to pinpoint the enemy weapons and Noble knew that time was against him. It was already half past five. He put his men under cover, except for Private Martin and another who manned a 2-inch mortar. Inevitably the two were dangerously exposed but very soon their mortar bombs, of which there were all too few, were whispering down into the enemy locality.

Under this covering fire Noble himself went out alone, carrying his only stretcher. He reached safely the area where the casualties lay and the first of the wounded that he saw was Kerr himself, severely hit but still giving out orders. His orderly, Fusilier Glennister, was with him and had patched him and others up as best he could with field dressings. A Bren-gunner was there too, still manning his weapon and all-set to fight to the last round. Noble and Glennister together got Kerr on to the stretcher, crawled away among the dead and wounded and carried him across the open paddy to safety, miraculously escaping the bursts of fire that the enemy put down.

Four more times Noble went out to the wounded, carrying them out on his back. All the time he was under fire from automatics and mortar bombs, which paused only when Martin's own mortar could effectively reply. Dusk had nearly fallen after his fifth trip, when he brought back the defiant Bren-gunner too. Simulated bird-calls and animal noises warned him that the Japanese were at their usual tricks of working round to trap him.

At that moment he was unexpectedly joined in the gloaming by a few men of 5 Troop, who included some walking wounded and a stretcher case who had become separated from the main force. By this time Sergeant Fred Slack had improvised some additional stretchers from bamboo and from the rifles of the dead. Together they set off in the dark on an agonizing march back, up and down the steep, wooded, trackless hills, the wounded on their makeshift stretchers crying at every jolt and stumble, the stretcher-bearers themselves exhausted and barely able to see their way.

But the stars shone out in all their tropic splendour when at last the little band, after more than one check, rejoined their Troop and began the journey back to Maungdaw. Pain and weariness were swallowed up in the pride of an exploit bravely conducted and in the warm commendations that followed. In this exploit Kerr's Troop had lost twenty-two men killed and fourteen wounded. A high price. More than half the Troop. But the guns were saved. Kerr himself lost an arm but won the Military Cross. Not surprisingly, Ray Noble also soon wore the same ribbon.

9

Screwdriver 2

At the time when, in their turn, the marine commando went in again to relieve their army comrades great changes were coming over the aspect of affairs. Away over on the main central front in Manipur, 300 miles away, the Japanese, giving voice to boastful slogans about 'marching on Delhi' (though their hard-headed generals had no intention of attempting any such thing) had begun their big *U-Go* offensive against 4th Corps in the mountains of Manipur. By the middle of March it had become apparent that the situation there was likely to develop into a decisive one and reinforcements for 4th Corps became an urgency. Slim, however, was in sore straits for trained divisions that were not earmarked for special purposes and he had already committed such as he had when Hanaya had launched his *Ha-Go* offensive against 7th Division in Arakan. This had been the very purpose of *Ha-Go*, so that, although it had been utterly crushed tactically, its strategic purpose had been achieved.

The Japanese, however, had this time reckoned without the resourcefulness of their adversary. Once more the imagination and initiative of Mountbatten were brought into play. He gave orders to hasten the reliefs of 5th and 7th Divisions by those already brought forward and he set in motion the bold and spectacular stratagem of sending Briggs and Messervy to Imphal by air complete. Thus began the most historic of 'air lifts', the first time ever that whole divisions – 'horse, foot and guns' – had been moved from one battlefield to another by air. To do this Mountbatten had to employ the hastiest of improvisations and to risk a rebuke from President Roosevelt by diverting American transport aircraft supplying the forces of Chiang Kai-shek beyond the 'Hump' of the Indo-Chinese mountain barrier.

F

Fifth Division began to pull out on 14 March, the day that, having captured Razabil, they had closed up to the western exit of the critical Tunnel. The exhausting operations and the intricate reliefs while in action went on for ten days and by the time that the marines sailed in again, Holmes's friends of the West Yorkshires had just left and the division's last brigade (Warren's 161st) were awaiting relief by units of Taffy Davies's 25th Division, under their badge of the Ace of Spades. British units of 36 Division were also concerned in the reliefs and for the next twelve days the operations on the sector South of Maungdaw were under the command of the impressive figure of Major-General Francis Festing. At the same period Lomax's 26th Division began to come back east of the hills to take over from 7th. The Corps, having now unlocked the outer baileys of the fortress, was bracing itself to break into the formidable keep.

As Denis Holmes looked out over the dehydrated paddyfields which had become his familiar stamping ground, grilling under a super-charged sun, and watched the arrival of the new faces coming in to replace old friends, he sensed the approach of a climax. The Arakan victory was in sight, but far away in the mountains of Manipur and the fortresses of Kohima a greater trial of strength had begun. As a distant flank to the British forces in that trial, Christison's corps had still an important mission to carry out. It was known that Hanaya was plotting a second offensive to regain the valuable ground that he had lost and Christison expected it to come in on the Maungdaw sector. So it was important that the harrying tactics of Operation 'Screwdriver' should be kept up with spirit and resourcefulness. For the same reason the eyes and ears of V Force, their value now thoroughly established, had become more than ever important and orders to all units on the Southern flank included specific instructions to maintain close contact with them. General Davies, very tall, very spare, very courteous, proved, when he took over from Festing on 4 April, to be no less aware of their value than Briggs and expressed his appreciation on the several occasions that he met Holmes.

It was in this setting that 44 (Royal Marine) Commando began the operation known as 'Screwdriver 2', strengthened in spirit and purpose by their first experiences. Cyril Horton had obtained Nonweiler's approval for a change of plan. The attempt to dominate the coastal plain from the hills had lacked a firm base, a secure line of supply and artillery support. All these requirements could be provided from the plain itself a little in advance of the troops already on the ground on the southern flank of 5th Division and their successors, now beginning to move in. Horton's orders from Nonweiler were to establish his headquarters at No-Can-Do, to operate on the divisional southern flank and to keep close contact with V Force. This plan gave great satisfaction not only to Horton but also to Holmes, who, in order to be close to the marines, established himself a mile and a half away in a tolerable hut at Ponra, the small, chaung-side Monk's Village with a pagoda and a smell of mud, where he enjoyed the shade of a grove of mangoes and where, guarded by a mangrove swamp in the rear, he could make a quick getaway by kisti. Before going in on the 21 March under the new divisional régime Horton had a talk with him and recorded that he found him 'amazingly well informed on Japanese movements' and having 'a keen insight into enemy reactions'. At Ponra Holmes had his first night in bed for eleven days and he spent all next day working on dreary accounts, while the fish-hawks wheeled overhead and the big butterflies flapped lazily to and fro.

Horton, apprehending the boxes of 5th Commando at Kanyindan and Dodan to be too vulnerable, secured Nonweiler's permission to abandon them and he spread out his Troops, each with its allotment of Holmes's scouts, among the villages from Lambaguna northwards, with his 3-inch mortars and Vickers machine-gun deployed in support. The marines, despite the ferocity of the sun, found their role very much to their liking. Among a friendly people they savoured the hot scents of the villages, admired the vivid birds and the gorgeous butterflies, listened to the shrill chorus of the multitudinous cicadas and, when they could, took refuge from the sizzling heat in the shade of the big banyans, mangoes and kanyin trees. In this phase they enjoyed also the strong support given them by Captain Graham, the gunner officer, who, on the very morning after the take-over, gave a most impressive demonstration of the accuracy of his 5·5-inch guns on a target south of Godusara.

What pleased Horton less was the unseamanlike behaviour of those who handled the river-craft that brought his men in by the long, tortuous, tidal chaungs which were the only means of approach and of subsequent supply. He recorded that they were 'lacking the most elementary knowledge of navigation', 'operated their craft as though they were road vehicles', 'got themselves stuck on mud-banks because they had no knowledge of the tides' and 'broached-to crab-fashion, sideways to the shore, so that they could not manœuvre'. It was unfortunate for these amateur sailors that they were now dealing with Royal Marines!

The return of the marines did not pass unnoticed by the alert enemy, who tuned in on Horton's radio, and, to the amusement of all at his headquarters, called them in excellent English, saying: 'We know you have returned, 44 Commando. But this time you will not be as fortunate as before, for we have brought up a large number of guns to blast you out.'

As if to implement this threat, the Japanese soon afterwards launched an attack on Lambaguna bridge, which had been a critical point throughout the whole of the 'Screwdriver' operations. Fortunately, Horton had been warned of the impending attack by V Force, who had reported the mustering of seventy Japanese at Hinthaya, a thousand yards away. Horton was thus able to reinforce his patrol at the bridge. A great crowd of natives from the villages around also congregated, eager to see the discomfiture of the yellow dogs. They were not disappointed. After a model little battle, in which the enthusiastic villagers joined by keeping up the supply of ammunition and even by steadying a light machine-gun firing from the top of a straw stack, the enemy were seen off, carrying six bodies with them.

At dusk the same day V Force scouts reported that the enemy were again mustering at Hinthaya and at 2.30 a.m. of a dark night the indications of a coming attack were unmistakable. The perils of a night attack were averted, however, by Graham's guns. Although the target had not been previously registered, an extremely accurate concentration of fire was brought down soon after the marines had signalled for support. The Japanese promptly scattered, taking to the hills, from which, as the villagers reported soon afterwards, they returned only to collect their casualties.

Two days later, again at dusk, the Japanese guns in the hills submitted the box which had been established near Lambaguna bridge to a light shelling, under cover of which infantry advanced close to the box and subjected it to heavy fire from machine-guns and grenades. Again the marines sent out their morse signal. Graham warned Horton of the danger of bringing down unregistered fire so close to our 'own troops', but Horton took the risk and again, before the enemy infantry could launch an assault, an accurate concentration of fire came down from the 5·5-inch guns, which sent the Japanese scuttling back to the hills.

It was a good beginning. Marines and villagers were alike exhilarated. Everywhere the natives extended them a welcome and a degree of hospitality which was almost embarrassing, offering succulent meals of chicken and rice to the patrols, with plentiful supplies of melons and entertaining their officers in the headmen's houses. Horton reported officially afterwards that, 'although their estimation of numbers was often exaggerated, the natives never failed to give accurate information of enemy movements'.

Such information was the basis of much of Horton's little campaign. Receiving daily reports from Holmes, he set out on a policy of raiding, luring and ambushing. Guided always by the V Force scouts in their stealthy way, his patrols went far and wide, from Alethangyaw northwards. He swapped his Troops around, to confuse the enemy's own spies. Holmes's scouts kept a special eye on the enemy parties that were always descending on the villages to commandeer rice and other foodstuffs, of which, under their bad administrative services, they had only a hand-to-mouth supply. They visited only those villages that they believed to be empty of British troops, so Horton, moving his patrols at night, was able to confront the enemy at dawn each day with a new and uncertain situation.

Again and again the enemy were taken by surprise. At Alethangyaw a patrol under Edward Sturges ambushed an enemy patrol, killing five and wounding two. At Hinthaya five were killed. At another village Oliver Hamlin met an enemy patrol, of which they killed eleven and wounded five. The gunners added their own substantial score, picking out gatherings of Japanese troops in the foot-hills.

These results, however, did not satisfy Horton and he entered upon the little Operation 'Snodgrass', in which an attempt was made to lure the enemy into the plain in large numbers, where the marines' machine-guns and mortars could take heavier toll. He moved his own headquarters to Lambaguna and re-deployed some of his Troops and sections. In daylight of 3 April, deliberately in full view of the enemy observation posts in the hills, he sent C Troop into Alethangyaw, hoping that the enemy would seize the opportunity of descending to cut them off in the rear, where Horton's other Troops were waiting. The Japanese did not respond to the invitation, but opened fire with 75-mm guns. Graham was asked if he could engage them and replied: 'Out of range, I'm afraid, but I might just reach them if we wait till midday, when the cartridge[1] will have got as warm as possible; that will give us just a bit of extra range.' He did so and got an apparent direct hit with his first shell, V Force reporting subsequently that the gun had been damaged and a Japanese officer killed.

While the marines were hunting and harrying the enemy, Holmes, besides feeding them with information, was also attending to what he called his Private Business. Anxious to extend still further the influence and contacts of his force, he paid visits to hitherto untried territory. One of these trips was to an important coastal village a full eight miles within enemy-dominated country named Myinhlut ('Loose Horse'), where he wanted to establish a new section of scouts. He took Habibullah with him (now proudly wearing a green beret on his shaggy head) and, with Horton's permission, was accompanied also by Captain Roger Steele.

They made the march by night, keeping to the white beach and meeting no enemy. At 'Loose Horse', while look-outs watched for a chance Japanese patrol, Holmes gave a talk to the village elders, who had been summoned by pre-arrangement. He urged them to have faith in an ultimate British victory, but

---

[1] The cartridge was the explosive charge that propelled the shell from the gun. The temperature of the charge affected the range of the gun.

counselled them to plough their rice fields and prepare for another monsoon of hardship. The British would not be able to get as far as Myinhlut before the monsoon, but then it would only be a matter of months before the people would again be 'under the government'.

Answering questions, he told them that the Japanese were lying when they said that they had captured Calcutta and that the British had been driven out of India. 'There are,' he said, 'a million British and Indian soldiers training there, ready for the final battles, and hundreds of thousands of soldiers from England are now fighting the enemy.'

The villagers entertained them hospitably in a fisherman's hut to a midnight meal of curried fish and rice and Holmes arranged to station a V Force section in the village. The party then marched back to Alethangyaw, where they were warned of a Japanese patrol in the town. Accordingly, they waited under cover while Habibullah made a quick reconnaissance. Holmes, feeling the need for rest and refreshment after their sixteen-mile march, made for Rob Roy's house and roused him from his sleep. The little agent gave them his spacious air-raid shelter for what was left of the night and brought them some hot tea, but urged them to move at daybreak.

When morning came they collected some fishing nets, walked coolly out to the beach, in full view of a knot of lounging Japanese soldiers, took a kisti and paddled safely home to Ponra, tired out.

A week later Holmes planned a visit for a similar purpose to the nearer village of Udaung ('Egg Hill'), when his scouts informed him that on a certain night a Japanese patrol was expected to arrive. 'Two birds with one stone,' he thought, and asked Horton for a raiding party. Horton gladly agreed and detailed Edward Sturges to lead it. The meeting with the headman having taken place, the patrol lay in ambush for the visiting enemy, but had the mortification to see them pass out of reach. As a small compensation, on the return journey the next night Holmes burned down the house of one Iman Sharif, notorious as an ally of the Japanese.

Ranging continually up and down the coast and inland nearly to the hills, Holmes had other irons in the fire also, including the constant business of sifting the reports of his scouts, interrogating suspects and visiting village headmen, sleeping in odd places and for four successive nights not sleeping at all. He was summoned to Maungdaw to see General Davies again, called on the commanders of the new brigades of 25th Division and allotted scouts to their units. He found Maungdaw 'shocking and full of dust, men and MT'.

On another of his hurried visits there he found that Mountbatten had arrived again, and he was hurriedly summoned to a parade of officers, all of whom were dressed in jungle green. Mountbatten, seeing a solitary figure in borrowed khaki shorts and shirt, not very smart, and wearing no badges of rank, asked Davies: 'Who is that queer-looking chap over there?' He had a long talk with Holmes about his work, finally telling him that it was time he went on leave, and left Holmes very much impressed by his invigorating presence.

A few days before two RAF Beaufighter sergeants, who had crashed in enemy country, had been rescued by a party of scouts under Yakub Boli, and Holmes was himself very soon to be immersed in a similar rescue attempt, which began just after the Udaung sortie and which will be one of the topics of the ensuing chapter.

That incident ended V Force's happy association with the eager young commandos, to whom, as to the Tarantulas, they had become very much attached. For the Commando Brigade was itself now to follow 5th and 7th Divisions to the Assam frontier on a mission of surveillance for the critical battle in which 4th Corps had now become locked. On 8 April orders arrived for the brigade to leave 'at once' and Nonweiler's headquarters and 5th Commando did so that same evening. The Marine Commando could not immediately disengage and, under the direct command of 25th Division, had to stay a few days longer, the final elements pulling out from No-Can-Do on the night of 12/13 April while Horton and his marines fumed and swore at the incompetence of the amateur sailors. It was this postponement that allowed Holmes to get help from the marines for the night march to 'Loose Horse' and for the sortie to 'Egg Hill'; it also allowed the marines themselves to give an unpleasant surprise to an extra strong Japanese patrol that came down from the hills to see if they were still there.

Before he left, Horton made the following official report:

Under the inspiring leadership of Major Holmes, the V Force organization was obviously exercising a very real influence not only on the morale and well-being of the native population, but on the course of operations as a whole. This was largely due to Major Holmes's personal example and disregard for danger. He worked in close co-operation with the officers of 44 (RM) Cdo and his reports were invariably well considered, although the degree of accuracy of his Intelligence did not appear to be fully appreciated by all those who received it. As in the case of the Burma Intelligence Corps Scouts, the V Force personnel quickly became an integral part of the sub-units to which they were attached. They earned the admiration of all ranks by the manner in which they performed their duties, whilst knowing full well the fate that awaited them if they fell into Japanese hands.

And later Horton wrote:

Major Holmes was brilliant in his appreciation of a situation, in his intuition for seizing an opportunity and in his insight into enemy reactions. He always seemed to be in the right spot at the right time. We should have been working in the dark without him and his brave scouts.

10

Private Enterprise

Silver Hill – The Rescue

The departure of the marines marked the end of a significant phase for the Western Mayu V Force. No longer were they allied with a particular band of brothers, but were to work in a rather more formalized way for whatever units of 25th Division might be in the front line. That front became contracted and offensive operations of any consequence seemed unlikely, though the main battle for the honeycombed mountain fastnesses of the Golden Fortress still raged beyond the ridge. No-Can-Do was garrisoned by fresh troops but the memory of the commandos remained with the scouts in the shapes of the green berets that crowned several swarthy heads.

They and their leader had to get to know a great many new faces and show them over the old ways, and were encouraged to find that the new faces were eager for their services. With the first rains not far off, the tropic sun waxed fiercer and fiercer and the humidity built up oppressively, overlaid with electrically charged pressures. The breath of a furnace blew in from the south-west and everybody stifled.

The night that the marines left was to be Holmes's last in his hut at Ponra, which he had been using as an advanced post and which he had deemed reasonably secure. He was very tired, after four nights without sleep, but the headman at Ponra had constantly advised him to move back north. Holmes was reluctant to do so, as he wanted to stay in close touch with No-Can-Do, but the headman now said to him:

'The *Japani* know you are here, sahib, and they would love to get you. You would be a great prize. I think they will raid this place very soon, as there are no British troops now to stop them.'

Jemadar Shaffi shared this opinion and when the news arrived from Rob Roy that the Japanese had tortured one of his informants, who had told them where the notorious V Force leader was, he decided that he must give way. There being no British troops on the mainland now south of Godusara, he moved back to his Dewdrop Inn at The Village of the Light of God, where he would be at the heart of the new operations.

The very night of his move (14 April) some twenty Japanese stealthily surrounded Ponra and rushed the vacated V Force huts. Finding the birds flown, they fired shots at random into the small neighbouring houses, wounding an old woman and two children, and set fire to Holmes's hut. Even before the next morning dawned Holmes received a detailed account of the raid.

Holmes saw the headman again a few days later and bluntly accused him of being a double agent. Taken aback, the headman answered: 'Yes, I may be, but please remember that I did warn you to leave before the *Japani* arrived. So at least I saved your lives.' He was a bit disgruntled that he was given a reward of only 100 rupees, but Holmes considered that that was all he was entitled to.

At Nurullapara, where he was to stay till the end, Holmes and his staff lived with some comfort, though not in complete safety. He had been extremely surprised when one day, entirely without warning, a smart contingent of six Gurkhas had arrived at Dewdrop Inn. The naik (corporal) in charge of them said that they had been sent to act as the major sahib's 'body-guard'. Holmes was amused, but perplexed to know what to do with them. So were the Gurkhas when Khyber Khan explained the major sahib's movements and the naik said complainingly:

'How are we to act as your bodyguard, sahib, if we never know where you are?'

Khyber, however, was delighted to have some soldiers to command at last and said:

'Never mind, sahib, I will detail their guard duties and instruct them in drill and musketry as we used to do in the 1st Punjabis. And perhaps, if Allah wills, they may have the chance to kill some *Japani*.' On one occasion they did.

There was a constant stream of visitors at Dewdrop Inn from the new division; all sorts of other people were wanting information and help of one kind or another or merely 'dropping in' for a social call. The diary records on the 15th: 'visitors every quarter of an hour'. But the host of Dewdrop Inn was not often there. Events crowded each other, one overlying another without respect to chronology. There was another long and chancy trip to 'Loose Horse'. There was a skirmish at Godusara between the Japs and a detachment of the 10th Baluch Regiment, which the diary described as 'great fun'.

The evacuation of much of the territory temporarily held by the commandos was the beginning of a period of anxiety for V Force. The Japanese had promptly gone in again and the scouts were very worried for the safety of their friends. An unholy band, headed by a Japanese Muslim known as Haji Ibrahim and a traitor ex-policeman from Singapore named Ghulam Ali began sniffing out all who had recently helped the British and preaching anti-British propaganda. Our own propaganda was not in evidence and the lack of it was not helped by the bombing of the wrong villages, as occurred at Godusara, where a strike by the Strategic Air Force caused the deaths of several villagers.

A few days after settling at the Village of the Light of God Holmes was joined by two valuable recruits. One was Captain Maurice Budd, who had been one of Firbank's dashing sailors-extraordinary, and the other was the marine Lieutenant Gus White, who had been sharply wounded at Alethangyaw. White had felt strongly drawn to V Force and Horton had given him his wish.

Holmes was quite delighted to have so valuable a recruit, for White was an ideal Intelligence officer, had heaps of guts and great personal charm. The diary records 'Gus a grand kid'. The scouts called him the 'Chota Sahib' (Little Master) by reason of his stature, youthful appearance, dark curly hair and ready smile. Holmes had given a promise to Horton that the Chota Sahib would not be involved in any dangerous or arduous mission until his wounds had fully healed.

Silver Hill

Very unexpectedly, some of Holmes's old friends in the Black Tarantulas reappeared upon the Western Mayu scene. The result was a difficult, dangerous and exhausting mission that occupied six days.

The Africans had been required by 26th Division, who had now replaced 7th, to make a reconnaissance of the Nanra area, close to the Nanra Pass of evil memory, which gave very rough access between the Naf and the Mayu across the hills. Nanra, lying on the eastern slope of the Mayus, was known or believed to be a Japanese advanced depot, but no information about it had been received for a long time. A prisoner was to be grabbed also if possible.

Such a task was out of the question from the eastern side, so the Tarantulas had at once thought of their old friends in the Western Mayu V Force, whom they knew to be masters in that sort of craft. Shattock, who was commanding, and Farquharson came over and asked Holmes to help them out on 16 April.

This was a damnably dangerous business. It meant going deep into the heart of the Mayu hills and penetrating into the jungle beyond, which was unknown to the Western Mayu team. It would mean trespassing on Anthony Irwin's territory, but Holmes did not think that that valiant officer would have any hard feelings.

As time pressed, Shattock quickly sent out a party under Lieutenant Ferguson, accompanied by V Force scouts, but they had to abandon it after a gallant attempt in the appalling hill country, where they apparently met opposition.

Meanwhile, Holmes had been consulting his scouts and as a result had planned an alternative route across the hills by an obscure and very difficult pass, known as the Ngewdaung (Silver Hill) Chaung, where a friend of Yakub Boli's lived. At this point the chaung cut through the hills between deep banks to empty itself on the eastern side into the Mayu River. It lay six miles to the north of the Nanra Pass and would mean a march, there and back, of forty miles, most of it over very rough country.

An indirect approach of this sort was typical of Holmes. He proposed to base himself on No-Can-Do, now garrisoned by a platoon of the East Lancashire Regiment under Lieutenant Glendenning, and march by way of his old beach route to Loose Horse. Silver Hill was quite outside the normal beat of

V Force, so Holmes first sent one of his scouts to the section at Loose Horse, with instructions to get all the 'gen' about the pass.

He set out from Dewdrop Inn on 16 April with a small party of African soldiers under the very tall figure of Lieutenant Freddie Gear, a born soldier, full of guts, accompanied by Shaffi and Yakub Boli. From No-Can-Do they marched by night with all due caution along the beach to Loose Horse, getting very wet as they forded the mouths of two chaungs. On arrival, the local scouts informed them that the Japanese were collecting a party of villagers at Silver Hill to cut bamboo early next morning and probably the following morning also, so the trip had to be put off. Holmes spent what was left of the night in the house of the local mulvi and the party returned to No-Can-Do the next night, having marched sixteen miles since the evening before.

After resting during the heat of the 18th, Holmes, Gear, Shaffi and Yakub Boli set off again the following evening, leaving the Africans behind on the strong advice of all the Chittagonians, who said that they would be far too conspicuous. The moon had declined, but the myriad stars that enamelled the velvet sky sufficiently illuminated the snow-white beach and the breakers that roared on their right hand. The sea breeze was invigorating after the hot breath of the day and there were no mosquitoes. Two and a half hours brought them, very wet, to Loose Horse, where the local scouts gave a favourable report on the situation at Silver Hill.

All in native dress, but the two officers wearing gym shoes, the party at once struck inland. From sea level they had a night climb before them of 1,100 feet. They were soon in very rough country, clambering among steep and wooded hills, following the courses of chaungs, often obstructed by huge boulders. The trees shut them in, occluding the stars. Perpetual night reigned here. The sweet sea-breeze had fainted away and gave place to the stink of rotting vegetation. The fidgety noises of jungle night life squeaked and rustled and jibbered around them, with an occasional uncanny scream as some unfortunate creature fell prey to another. What was five miles on the map became three hours of clambering in the hot, fretful dark.

At the end of that time, Yakub, who led throughout, said that they were near to the house of his friend on the Silver Hill chaung, so he and Shaffi advanced silently to reconnoitre and to see Yakub's friend. They returned with news that a party of Japanese soldiers was spending the night in the pass, close to the chaung. Questioning Yakub, Holmes learnt that the banks of the chaung were fairly high and fringed with bamboo. Would these bamboos, Holmes asked, hide the chaung from the *Japani*? Yes, they would; the *Japani* were encamped on a track above.

'Very well, Freddie,' Holmes said. 'We go up the chaung itself. Hope you can swim.'

They crept forward in the dark from tree to tree and entered the swirling waters of the chaung, having some two hundred yards to go to reach the farther side of it. Very soon the water was over Holmes's shoulders and he whispered to Gear: 'If you were my height, Freddie, you'd know now what it means to be "up to your neck in it".'

Thus they safely evaded the sleeping Japanese above them and at last came out on the eastern side, but, as they scrambled out of the chaung, their lungyis and shirts dripping, they only just avoided a Japanese soldier who coughed a few yards away and appeared to be patrolling a track. The darkness of the night was now welcome but it was fearfully hot and damp and the thorns of the thick jungle scratched and tore them as they crept through. The sweat was making streaks down the black camouflage cream that coated their faces, arms and legs. They scrambled down the steep and rocky jungle on the east side and at 4 a.m. found some dense cover and went to sleep.

At dawn they crept from their cover and beheld a splendid panorama below them, with the Mayu River glistening four miles away. As they crouched, a Jap patrol slipped by only a few yards from them. Cautiously they turned right towards Nanra, along the shoulder of the hills, Yakub and Shaffi always in the van. There was ample cover. In the country below them they saw plenty of Japs and hungered after a prisoner. They had a quick snack of biscuits and water and presently came to a broad, well-used path; this, Yakub said, was the track into the Nanra Pass, which Tanahashi had used the year before to surprise 6th British Brigade. Avoiding the path, the party turned downhill towards Nanra, which they saw as a widely spread group of bashas. The going was very steep and severe, the sun fiercely hot now, so that they were all bathed in perspiration.

Gear studied Nanra through his field-glasses and said that he saw no sign of movement. Holmes ordered a halt 500 yards short of the place and sent Yakub and Shaffi forward. They returned to say that the place was completely empty and riddled with bomb holes. Holmes said: 'Well, that's that, Freddie. Useful information for your Div.'

They turned back to Silver Hill, taking careful notes about what little they could see of the enemy. Their thoughts now turned to bagging a prisoner, but they had no luck. They felt sure of a victim on the track to the Nanra Pass and set an ambush, two on each side of the path, but no one passed. Evening drew on. They thought of going farther downhill, where plenty of Japs were to be seen in the distance, but what they needed was a single man, or possibly two, whom they could quickly and quietly overcome. Holmes decided that they had done all they could. On top of the previous night's climb, they had walked and scrambled twelve miles that day and their food was nearly exhausted; so were they.

On the afternoon of the 20th, having covered twenty-eight miles of very tough country, they were back at No-Can-Do utterly worn out.

Though they had not been able to snatch a prisoner, they were able to send back some very useful information, including the locations of a Japanese observation post and three defensive positions. Holmes wrote in his diary:

'What a night . . . Yakub and Shaffi were marvellous.'

The Rescue

The reconnaissance for the Tarantulas interrupted a long sequence of attempts, extending over more than a fortnight, to rescue another RAF pilot in distress. Subsequently his identity was established as Warrant Officer John R. G. Campbell, of the Royal New Zealand Air Force, attached to No. 258 Squadron, RAF.

On or about 2 April, while flying very low over the Mayu

River, he had struck the mast of a rice boat and had crashed in flames in the river. He had succeeded in extricating himself with only minor injuries and had swum to the west bank. There he had been set upon by hostile Mughs, who had stripped him of his effects, including his escape gear. They had then let him go and he had made his way through the jungle and across the spine of the Mayu hills to the western side, where, at Donbaik, which was an enemy headquarters, he had run into a Japanese patrol. In the dark he had eluded them, however, and had gone into hiding in a bamboo thicket near Thawin Chaung, the very same village where 'P. O. Thompson' had taken refuge. There he had been found, befriended and concealed by the Muslims. Word had been sent to the section of V Force scouts at Loose Horse, who had at once sent off a messenger to Holmes.

The news reached Holmes on 10 April, the morning after he and Edward Sturges had returned to Ponra from the abortive night sortie on Udaung. As in the case of Thompson, Holmes's first action was to send the scout back with a message to stay where he was at all costs. It was to be another case of Private Enterprise.

He then immediately organized a rescue force. From Binks Firbank he borrowed a motor launch, captained by Charles Cornish, and from Cyril Horton he secured a small squad of Royal Marines under Edward Sturges, accompanied by Tony Macan. The party set out from No-Can-Do on the night of 11 April under a full moon, towing a kisti, but ran into trouble after about twelve miles, when (Cornish having no map!) the ship struck a rock in dangerous waters. She soon developed a list on the port bow. With every wave there was a horrible crunching sound. Water slopped into the engine room. The Bengali crew lost their heads and threw up their arms. The engine-room hands ran up on deck to add to the panic, leaving the engine running and the screw whirring in the air. On all sides there were cries of 'Allah! Allah!' Holmes was instinctively reminded of the panicky disciples on the Lake of Galilee crying: 'Master, master, we perish.'

Cornish was at his wits' end to control them. Hands were already beginning to abandon ship. To add to the predicament,

G

a Japanese post ashore had seen them in the bright moonlight and began to open fire with a machine-gun. The rounds fell far short but the anxiety was not lessened.

At this juncture Sturges took charge and his marines quietly displaced the frightened Bengalis on deck and in the engine room. Sturges ordered 'Full astern' and the ship lifted easily off the rocks and righted herself at once. The serang, or native boatswain, took heart and rallied his hands. Allah had indeed answered their prayers.

The ship proceeded on course and a little later the kisti was put ashore to recover Campbell, only to find that it was the wrong place. The attempt was abandoned. Cornish turned to starboard and made for Coconut Island out in the bay. Thence Holmes went over to Ponra for his last night there. He was feeling dead-beat, his diary saying: 'Feeling very tired; this my fourth night in succession with no sleep.' But he found Bernard Shattock and Jack Farquharson, of the West Africans, waiting to see him about the Silver Hill affair and he had to say good-bye to the marines before moving himself back to Dewdrop Inn at the Village of the Light of God.

For two days he became immersed in matters of immediacy as the patrols of 74 Brigade began moving and then he was off on the expedition to Silver Hill; but he left instructions to his officers – Budd, White and 'Martin' Luthera – to lay on another attempt to rescue Campbell. White sent off two or three messages concealed in cigarettes, but Campbell was a non-smoker and never investigated the cigarettes. He sent back one of the emptied packets, however, on which he had scribbled a little message that Budd and White found peculiarly touching; it said simply:

'Am OK and waiting for you.'

After the exhausting affair of Silver Hill Holmes got himself and Shaffi ferried over on 21 April for a brief rest in the idyllic beauty of Coconut Island, where they found the white beach thickly carpeted with red crabs. The islanders welcomed them with a splendid repast of rice, fish, fresh fruit and the milk of coconuts. Gus White was there as well, but the sweetness of the holiday air and the freshness of the sea-breeze that tempered the ferocity of the tropic sun were to be embittered as they ruefully witnessed the failure of two more attempts to reach the unfortunate Campbell.

One was made the same night on the generous and gallant initiative of the islanders themselves, prompted by Shaffi. Accompanied by the jemadar and young Habibullah, they set out in a long kisti and began the difficult thirteen miles passage across the bay with no moon and a rising sea. The villagers said prayers for them, in which Holmes and White joined in spirit. The prayers were indeed needed, for the signs were unpropitious. At that time of year the river mouths of the Arakan coast act as funnels for the south-west 'chota monsoon' wind and navigation for any kind of small craft is dangerous. When the long kisti was but half-way across the bay a strong wind on the starboard beam lashed the water. The little craft all but capsized several times. Forced to bale out continuously, hands had little time for manning the paddles. Habibullah was violently sick. Campbell's luck was out again.

Meanwhile, as Holmes's deputy, Maurice Budd had been active and had collected together from various sources a well-planned expedition, which arrived at the island later that day, the 22nd. Binks Firbank had lent him *Torotua*, the ship that had been Budd's own command before he joined V Force. Very wisely, in view of the navigational hazards and the difficulty of locating Thawin Chaung in the dark, Budd had also enlisted Lieutenant James Colquhoun of the Bengal Pilotage Service, together with an RAF doctor, another RAF officer, Luthera and some official photographers (Captain Boon Houston and Sergeant A. Salem) of the Public Relations Film Unit, hopeful of getting some exciting pictures. The affair had stirred the sporting interest of everyone at Maungdaw and General Davies had ordered that V Force was to have every help.

Full of promise, the expedition set out that same night on the third attempt, but once again there was a miscarriage. Experienced pilotage took them safely to the right place, but could not get *Torotua* inshore in face of the formidable surf at the mouth of the Thawin Chaung and apparently no landing craft was carried that was capable of surmounting it.

Everyone was very glum. The island air suddenly seemed to turn sour, the white beach to become changed to ashes, the

coconut palms to droop in despondency. V Force felt that their
honour was at stake and Holmes determined to go on trying.
Torotua having been required to return to Maungdaw, he took
passage in her and, wearing a lungyi, shirt, gym shoes and nine
days' beard, presented himself to Taffy Davies, who promised
him the help of Lt-Colonel Featherstonhaugh, commander of
one of the larger Water Transport units.

Davies asked him: 'When will you be ready to have another
go?'

'At once, sir.'

'You must have a night's sleep first. And get rid of that
shocking beard. I will tell Colonel Featherstonhaugh to be
ready at eight o'clock tomorrow morning.'

Holmes was very grateful but not wholly satisfied. He had
made a little plan in his mind and paid one or two more calls before borrowing a jeep and running himself down the hot and dusty
track to Dewdrop Inn. He shaved, looking aghast at his image
in the mirror as he scraped off the remainder of the black camouflage cream still clinging to his beard. Towards evening he was
distressed when one of his scouts from Loose Horse arrived with
a pathetic little message from Campbell, saying simply:

'Please come quickly.'

He questioned the scout, who told him that a Japanese
patrol was beating the country round about and questioning
everybody in their search for the pilot, but that the villagers
were keeping a careful eye on the patrol and were ready to move
Campbell at a moment's notice. Tomorrow, thought Holmes,
we've damned well got to pull it off. Then, for the first time in
nine nights, he tumbled into his bed.

Featherstonhaugh sailed down to Coconut Island next day,
the 25th, in his *Stella* and Holmes sailed with him. It was
apparent to Holmes, as it must have been to everyone, that the
real problem was the heavy surf on the beach. *Stella* was no
answer to this. Holmes had therefore asked Shaffi to produce
from somewhere a really strong craft rigged with sails, so, on
arrival at the island, he was relieved when the smiling and
resourceful jemadar met him to say that he had borrowed a
fine sailing kisti belonging to his relative Abu Soolay.

Holmes intended this kisti to be manned, not by the local

fishermen but by resolute men picked from among his own scouts, accompanied by a guide from Thawin Chaung. After consultation with Featherstonhaugh, the plan made was that, the wind being favourable, the kisti should sail over alone, but that *Stella* should follow and, after arrival off the farther coast, stand out to sea to pick up the rescue party. If the surf was too rough for the kisti, two good swimmers were to be launched and secured by log lines. If more than one attempt was necessary, it would be made at all hazards and Holmes offered a reward of 1,000 rupees (about £75) if Campbell was got out safely. Every V Force officer was eager to lead the rescue party, none more so than Holmes. He realized, however, that he was still very fatigued and decided that they should draw lots for the leadership. The choice fell upon Luthera. He could not swim, but did not disclose the fact.

The little ship's company assembled on the beach towards evening, before the raised eyebrows of the spectators from upriver, who thought that they looked like a gang of desperadoes. Besides Shaffi, the crew included 'Scarface', a villainous-looking fisherman from Loose Horse, red-lipped from the juice of the betel-nut, the stern, black-bearded Siddiq, the long-haired, grinning Harpo Marx, his comical hat replaced by a commando's green beret, and the grisled Yakub Boli, looking every inch a wrestler. Even their leader seemed cut from the same buccaneering pattern; for Luthera, reverting to traditional Sikh custom, had now grown long hair and a black, bushy beard, so that, in his lungyi like the rest, he looked as piratical as any. As if to give further notice of a desperate intent, all wore Mae Wests.

Featherstonhaugh, regarding them sceptically, could hardly believe that this was intended to be a serious operation of war. Holmes remarked to him:

'Hollywood would pay plenty of money for that lot, sir.'

Featherstonhaugh grunted and answered:

'I can't see that gang being of the slightest use. Still, let's wish them luck.'

Holmes shook hands with the smiling Luthera, saying: 'Good hunting, Martin. Bring him back alive.'

From the deck of *Stella* they watched the gallant little ship

set sail with a following wind about an hour before dark. A
little knot of islanders had gathered on shore also. The declining
sun seemed to focus on her for a while. Then she slipped into the
gathering gloom and was lost. Two hours later *Stella* weighed
and followed.

There was no moon that night. Holmes, watching with White
from the deck of *Stella* the flickering phosphorescence on the
water, saw with relief that the wind and the sea had moderated.
He knew that the kisti would take some three hours to make the
crossing and that their first difficulty, with no navigational aids
of any sort, was to maintain the right course and to identify the
mouth of the chaung in the dark. The Arakan boatmen had a
very shrewd sense in such matters and he assumed that they
would make an approximate landfall and then work along the
coast until they found their objective by visual recognition. The
suspense of the night increased when at last the Mayu coast became dimly visible and *Stella* was brought to dead slow. With the
ship darkened, all on board waited in anxious silence, watching
and listening to whatever might come out of that hostile shore.

Meantime, unseen by anyone, Luthera's little party had
triumphantly overcome all fears and misgivings. The surf had
mercifully abated somewhat. As planned, the prow of the kisti
was pointed a few hundred yards away from the chaung,
where the enemy might be less likely to be on the watch. She
rode easily, rising to the swell. Very soon she felt the first
breakers beneath her, creaming along her dug-out hull.
Another moment and the breakers were rearing high, drenching
them with wind-whipped spray. Then, quite suddenly, guided
by skilful hands, she was up, over and through, lying safely on
the beach.

Shaffi's smile gleamed in the night as he said quietly to
Luthera: 'Allah be praised, sahib. The waves were our only
enemy. Now we shall bring back the British airman safely.'

Led by the local guide, he and another scout moved warily
along the dark beach towards the chaung. Within an hour they
were back, trimphantly carrying the distressed pilot. Faint and
feeble, he spoke few words as Luthera greeted him. The kisti
was turned about and launched, but now had to fight a harder
battle against a stiffening wind and more threatening breakers.

She became waterlogged and hands were soon wet through and hard put to keep her baled out and hold a course with the paddles. At last they were safely through by resolute effort, but made slow progress against the now adverse wind until at last, after half an hour's arduous paddling, they discerned the dark shape of *Stella*.

Luthera shone a torch and the tiny pinpoint was quickly spotted by the anxious watchers on board. Featherstonhaugh changed course to meet her and, as they closed, those on board the launch could hear the sound of excited voices that seemed to speak clearly of success. As Campbell was brought on board Featherstonhaugh could hardly believe his eyes. 'Absolute miracle,' he remarked.

Campbell turned out to be a small, pale, emaciated figure in a ragged shirt and lungyi. He was skin-and-bones, light as a feather and his flesh as white as a plucked chicken's. He was about twenty years of age, but only a few hairs on his chin gave evidence of some twenty-four days without benefit of razor. The local Chittagonians, at great risk to themselves, had watched over him devotedly, concealing him with expert craft in dense vegetation, from which he had been unable to move except at night. Keeping stealthy watch on the Japanese patrols, they had fed him regularly on rice and dried salt fish, a diet that had at first made him very sick but to which he had become accustomed.

The diary proclaims triumphantly: 'WE GOT HIM!' The RAF doctor took charge of Campbell and all returned in *Stella* to Maungdaw. Holmes, Luthera, Campbell and one or two others, all looking like the most sinister of cut-throats and becoming the target of all eyes, walked to 25th Division headquarters, where they were promptly arrested by the military police. However, General Davies, having been informed, himself came out from a commander's conference that he was conducting and heartily congratulated the ragged and dishevelled gang. Afterwards Holmes took them all down to Dewdrop Inn at the Village of the Light of God, where there was a great party and where Campbell had a bath, a shave and a change of clothing before being handed over to the Royal Air Force.

It had all been another triumph for Private Enterprise.

11

The Demon's Turban

The last scene opens. The first 'mango rains' have burst, the first mango fruits have fallen and the full monsoon, which will bring all serious fighting to a stop, is due to burst in May.

Gradually, one by one, painfully, heroically, the British and Indian troops were storming the fortified eagle's nests clustered on the last pinnacles of the Golden Fortress. Now, at the end of April, the sweating troops of Lomax's 26th Division, shouldering the heavy pressure of the pre-monsoon heat, bent their backs to the steep uprising of the last of all the craggy, jungle-clad summits – the T-shaped Point 551. The Japanese, who might have been thought impregnable in such lofty fastnesses, resisted with all their customary determination, but were gradually outfought by better troops, splendidly led, physically tough, who now demonstrated their hard-learned lessons of close and intimate co-ordination of all arms even at the bayonet's point.

In 25th Division's territory on the western coastal plain that bordered the Naf, the bickering still continued briskly in the heat and sweat and dust, each side a little nervous of a flanking thrust by the other. To V Force the abandonment of the country won in 'Screwdriver' was a sad event and their thoughts dwelt with anxiety upon the fortunes of all those villagers who had so selflessly befriended them.

Denis Holmes, ensconced in the Village of the Light of God, and wearing the minimum of clothing, lived a double life on the heady fringes of the battlefront, within smell of the enemy but comfortably bedded down and enjoying the company of a steady stream of visitors of all sorts from both sides of the line. Dewdrop Inn, now staffed with four officers, resembled a miniature information headquarters, with an impressive map room presided over by the little Interpreter Shaffi, now a very knowledgeable Intelligence Officer. The six little Gurkhas kept guard within and without the compound and Khyber Khan reigned firmly as major-domo of the establishment.

The little Force worked hand-in-glove with 25th Division; a liaison officer from the brigade in the line (now Angus's 51st, now Hirst's 74th) called daily at Dewdrop Inn for the latest information, and the brigade commanders themselves occasionally 'dropped in'. Holmes was delighted to find that the brigade-major of 51st was Rex Clifford, an officer of his own battalion, who had seen a great deal of active service and who was later to become his second-in-command when Holmes himself commanded the battalion in Italy.

From the enemy side, numbers of disillusioned Jiffs also drifted in disconsolately to surrender themselves. One of these was recognized by Kaloo the Killer as the murderer of a villager in Alethangyaw. Out flashed Kaloo's knife. He leapt forward and struck, but the presence of mind of the British interrogating officer saved the Jiff from anything more serious than a gash in the shoulder. From other Jiffs it was learnt that the Japanese had again circulated Holmes's name and description with a reward for his capture. Holmes had a good laugh and suffered having his leg pulled by allusions to *The Police Gazette*.

From Dewdrop Inn parties of the enemy were seen moving in the heavily wooded country to the east and occasionally there was a light brush with them, as when 'Johnnie', who had worked here with the West Yorkshires, led out a party of scouts in a light-hearted chase of a Japanese patrol, shooting off their newly acquired rifles with amateur abandon.

V Force had firmly established itself as one of the most reliable links in the Intelligence chain. Looking back to that momentous first day of 1944, Holmes and his friends could not fail to be struck by the enormous advance that had been made in the standing of the Force. Then it had been regarded, at best, with a kindly tolerance; as a bunch of well-meaning amateurs to be treated with indulgence but not to be relied upon. Today, by contrast, they were an indispensable element of the forward troops, trusted for their reliability and called upon daily for their help. On the Western Mayu this transformation, under the active encouragement of the senior commanders, had been primarily brought about by the initiative, daring and unresting energy of Denis Holmes. Yet it was at this moment that something occurred which caused a complete revulsion in his feelings.

He received a summons to attend a meeting at Bawli Bazar to discuss the future of V Force and, somewhat distrustful, went there in a light truck on the last day of April. The first of the monsoon storms had just broken, laying the abominable dust and mercifully dispelling the sultry air of the past few weeks, but turning everything into mud. The sounds of the great battle behind him were smothered in the cannon-fire of the rain as Holmes's truck splashed along the road. Arriving at Bawli in the deluge, he was in no great humour and what he had to listen to at the ensuing conference did nothing to improve it. 'Rock-bound' Donald, having been too outspoken to a general, had gone and the whole atmosphere of the place had changed. What he had to listen to filled Holmes with disgust and at the end of the day he entered in his diary: 'Frightful farce.'

Worse was to follow when the conference resumed the next day.

To Holmes's mind, certain of the new men seemed quite unsuitable. Their ideas of how best to serve the fighting divisions were not his. Was the show now going to be run by the methods of base-wallahs with no relish for the cannon's mouth? Were they trying to build a new 'empire' for themselves alone?

We need not, after the years, go into all his doubts and fears, nor whether in the event they were to be justified or disproved; perhaps they were exaggerated because he felt angry and offended. He was by nature modest, but no one could deny that it was he who had made a success of the Western Mayu V Force and he felt that his way of doing things had been amply proved to be the right way for the fighting soldier.

As he listened to these plans unfolding he reflected that the last few months had been the happiest of his life. He had lived among good friends, had tasted danger and fatigue with them, shared their triumphs, joined in their laughter and had felt enriched by their high spirits. He had been virtually his own master. Life had been an adventure and in adventure he had found a mission peculiarly his own. He would hate to leave all that behind and hate to part from his faithful scouts. But he saw that in the proposed new régime nothing would be the same again. The old 'magic' would vanish. And, after all, the campaign in Arakan was almost over and there would be very little work of real importance for him to do in the monsoon.

These thoughts in their turn brought him sharply also to a realization that the leadership of an irregular band of scouts was doing nothing to further his career as a professional soldier. Men who were his juniors were being advanced, while he had stood still; had, in fact, been stepped down for a period, for the Babus back in India had stopped his pay as a major, since V Force had no authorized 'establishment'. Rex Clifford and others of his old friends were saying to him: 'Why don't you go back to the Regiment? They want you.'

So it was with mixed feelings that, on 1st May, he entered starkly in his diary:

'Decided to finish with V Force.'

However, the time was not yet. When he arrived back at the compound of Dewdrop Inn that night, he was greeted by Gus White with news that jerked him back to his normal optimism. There was one more task to do, one more little battle to fight, one more chance to strike a blow at the enemy and to prove that his methods were right.

The extreme southern sector of the front, where Dewdrop Inn stood, looking at the tree-clad foot-hills where the enemy lurked, was held by the 6th Battalion of the Oxfordshire and Buckinghamshire Light Infantry (usually shortened to the 'Oxfords' or the 'Ox and Bucks') under Lt-Colonel Metcalfe. A strong friendship quickly developed between them and V Force; a patrol which Metcalfe established at Godusara called at Dewdrop Inn every evening. The Oxfords were a young, fit and keen lot, eager to get at the enemy, but under some restraint through shortages in their ranks, from which most units from Britain were now suffering.

News had recently come of a northward movement by Japanese troops towards Godusara and a minor 'flap' had ensued. The simple facts were that the Japs had occupied a little wooded hamlet called Thayegonbaung ('the Turban of the

Demon'), just north of Lambaguna, and had constructed two strong works. A platoon from another battalion, with Budd as their chief V Force aide, had recently gone to attack the position, but had run into trouble and become involved in a roughhouse before extricating themselves. The Oxfords in their turn were now anxious to root out what might become a dangerous growth and had asked for the help of V Force.

The original information had come from an agent named Yusuf, whom Holmes knew to be reliable, but, after White had told him about the affair, it was clear to him that, if another attempt was to be made, a close and detailed reconnaissance was necessary. It would be a dangerous job, so, after a talk with Metcalfe, he decided to go himself. It would blow away the dust and ashes in his mouth after the Bawli visit and it held out hopes for one last little adventure. He took White and Shaffi with him and, wearing lungyis, they went out on the night of 4 May. As he had so often done before, he avoided the short direct route of only three and a half miles and, enjoying once more the smell of the sea, took a very roundabout one by river to No-Can-Do and Ponra by way of the Ton Chaung and thus approached Thayegonbaung from the rear under a gibbous moon.

To Holmes and Shaffi poignant memories returned as they entered this familiar old stamping ground. Their kisti crept cautiously past the dark mangrove swamp and up the muddy water that led to Ponra, and there, silhouetted against the night sky on the bank above them, stood the charred remains of the old hut from which he had escaped only just in time. There also, by pre-arrangement, they picked up a local guide lurking in the moon shadows named Abdul, a sinister-looking fellow whose face had been scarred by a Japanese bayonet. He had a fierce hatred for the Japs, who had abducted his son's wife and had slashed his face when he had tried to resist and had then burnt his house down. Abdul knew the enemy dispositions at the Demon's Turban exactly and was burning to see the 'yellow dogs' put to the sword.

Since White was not yet fit, Holmes sent him back in the kisti. He and Shaffi then landed quietly among some muddy mangroves and, led by Abdul, went ghost-like by old, familiar ways across dark, freshly ploughed paddy-fields, avoiding

Lambaguna and seeing not a soul, and so, sweating profusely, beheld the Demon's Turban sleeping under the moon. Here Abdul led them to a small copse of betel-palms that gave them good cover about two hundred yards from the target and there they lay up till daylight.

It was not long before the sun's huge brazen ball gleamed above the Mayu hills, and, while the western slopes still lay in their own black shadow, shot its fiery rays upon the plain. The earth soon roasted, the cicadas began their chitinous whine and the flamboyant butterflies flapped lazily here and there. The Japanese emerged to go about their business, their incessant chatter audible even at that distance. Holmes and his companions ate and drank a little, then Holmes glued his field-glasses to his eyes off-and-on for a couple of hours, while Abdul pointed out the features detail by detail, interspersing his exposition with muttered imprecations and with admonitions to Holmes to wipe out the infidel dogs.

'Not one of them must be left alive, sahib,' he said.

Shaffi's smile gleamed with approval as he remarked: 'Abdul speaks well, sahib.'

What Holmes saw was a dual position. The larger of the two, manned by about forty Japanese, consisted of bunkers and bashas very well sited on high ground surrounded by mango trees. About a hundred yards to the west was a smaller bunker within the compound of a solitary basha set among some betel-palms and having a long, narrow trench extending outside the compound. This second position was manned by about a dozen men and it contained also a crow's nest built in a high tree above the basha. A sentry was clearly seen in the crow's nest and Abdul told them that it was manned day and night. Holmes observed, however, that it did not look to the rear. The two positions were connected by a deep trench and each was commanded by an officer. A telephone line, Abdul reported, ran to gun positions in the hills behind. Altogether, Holmes judged, it was quite a tough nut to crack; it would mean an attack by at least a full company of infantry, supported by artillery. Not an operation to be undertaken lightheartedly.

He and Shaffi had now to make their getaway. Holmes, feeling a compelling urgency for quick action, decided that it should be by the direct route on foot, which could be covered in an hour or so. In the brilliant sunlight, with the enemy only two hundred yards away, this was going to be tricky, but fortune favoured them. Holmes was just wondering what to do when Shaffi said: 'Look, sahib, there's a herd of cattle over there. It looks as though it's coming our way.'

It was. The three men casually mingled with the beasts until they were well beyond the range of Japanese eyes. Then Abdul went home, with instructions from Holmes for another rendez-vous that night.

Holmes was acting under a strange compulsion and felt a resurgence of the sense of magic that had animated the earlier raids. He wanted a battle, he wanted to be right in it and wanted it quickly. It would be his last with V Force. Then he would get away at once. He must somehow persuade Metcalfe to attack the place without delay and thought that that would be easy, for the Oxfords' CO was clearly a man of mettle. So, passing through the safety of Godusara, he went straight to Metcalfe's HQ and found that Brigadier Hirst, commander of 74th Brigade, was there also. To both of them he explained the situation and tentatively suggested a plan.

As he expected, Metcalfe was eager to attack that very night and Hurst gave his approval, qualified by a warning against incurring heavy casualties. Holmes was delighted; he already had had a night without sleep, but feared that any delay might result in the chance for a fight being lost.

Metcalfe's orders were for the attack to be made by one company, with a second company in reserve. Both enemy positions were to be attacked simultaneously. The larger position was identified as Mango Clump and the smaller as Betel Hut. Artillery support was to be on call from Metcalfe's command post, which would be south of Godusara.

In conformity with this plan, Holmes allotted his guides. He decided to do the thing in style this time and use all his best men. He knew perfectly well that his duty required him to do no more than provide men who would guide the assaulting troops to the right place and even that was scarcely necessary in the circumstances; but he saw the chance of a tough little battle, and he intended to be in on it. So, with Metcalfe's approbation, he detailed himself and Habibullah to accompany the smaller party of No. 14 Platoon, which was to attack Betel Hut, and he gave Maurice Budd and Jemadar Shaffi to the other two platoons for their attack on Mango Clump. Another of his scouts he sent to cut the enemy's telephone lines.

Having sent off two or three other scouts to make certain arrangements, Holmes snatched a few hours' sleep in the torpor of the afternoon, then changed into uniform and by 7 o'clock of 5 May, when it was fully dark, was on his way with No. 14 Platoon. It was commanded by a young subaltern named Bisley, who was conspicuous for both his height and his monocle, and who impressed Holmes at once by his competence and fine bearing and the strong bond of confidence between him and his men. Marching quietly along in the hot night with these young men and chatting occasionally to them in a low voice, Holmes, who had not been home for several years, thought that, if all the youth of England were like these, there was nothing much wrong with the old country.

Bisley, of course, was in command, but naturally leaned much upon the experience of his 'guide'. On Holmes's advice, the platoon had been directed to make the indirect approach that he always favoured, so that the enemy could be taken from the rear, which they always disliked. He had chosen again a route via Ponra, where Abdul was to meet them and where a fleet of sampans would quietly take them as near as possible to their objective. The main party, for the attack on Mango Clump, was to march more directly due south by the main road. 'Divide to march, unite to fight.'

Embarked at Ponra, Bisley's platoon glided forward to the appointed disembarkation point, where Holmes left the boats in White's charge, in obedience to the promise given to Horton that White should not be given any dangerous mission until his wound was properly healed. By midnight, led by Abdul, whose whole being was tense with suppressed excitement, Bisley's platoon was on the designated assault line, with the betel-palms dimly visible. Holmes reckoned that from their rear and flank position they would be undiscerned by the lookout man in the crow's nest. No moon was yet to be seen. They had a little time to wait. All the world except themselves seemed to be asleep.

Abdul was now due to make contact with the main force marching from Godusara and point out to them the details of their target at Mango Clump; but before moving away he said to Holmes, tapping the long *dah* strapped to his lungyi and his voice strong with emotion:

'Sahib, I beg you to leave just one yellow dog alive, so that I can revenge myself with this.'

Bisley made a neat little plan for his platoon to attack in two small 'waves' of about a dozen men each. The first, led by Bisley himself, would attack from one side under a smoke-screen from the 2-inch mortar and under covering fire from the second wave. The second wave would then make for the communicating trench between the two positions, to prevent the escape of the Betel Hut garrison. Bisley had no second officer to command this little wave, so he asked Holmes if he would do so and Holmes needed no persuading. He felt curiously elated and light of heart, as though at a holiday gathering, and was inspired by a sense of complete and happy concord with these keen, trustful and thoroughly likeable young Englishmen. He was glad to be leading troops again, especially ones so willing to be led. It was, indeed, the first time that he had ever led British troops and felt that he could do anything with them and lead them anywhere.

The time was 12.45, the night warm but with that gentle breeze from the sea that he had always liked. Bisley quickly passed the order to fix bayonets – that dramatic order which makes men hold their breath a little – then gave the order for smoke. As the mortar bombs burst and their smoke billowed out, the Oxfords could clearly hear the Japanese calling out in alarm and confusion. They did not know what was happening nor where the attack was coming from. Before they could collect themselves the hand grenades were bursting among them from a few yards range, followed immediately by the rush of bayonets materializing frighteningly in the dark.

On the left Holmes's group moved off with perfect timing. The Regular Indian Army officer found himself instinctively talking to these young Englishmen as though they were all schoolboys together going to a football match. His only order to them was a quiet and utterly unmilitary:

'Come on, chaps, let's go.'

They went, and to some purpose. In a few minutes the Betel Hut position was in British hands and cut off from Mango Clump. In the still lingering smoke Holmes went to meet Bisley and found that the tall young man completely composed, monocle still glued to his eye, briskly reorganizing for counter-attack. Holmes said:

'Good show, old boy.'

Bisley smiled and Holmes could swear that he flushed with pleasure as he answered: 'Thank you, sir, but it was the chaps, not me.'

'That's what Wellington said. Anyhow, you look as though you had just scored a try for England.'

'Feel a bit like that, sir; what do we do now?'

'Better count the score.'

They found nine dead Japanese and a tenth who would not last long. Bisley's losses had been one soldier killed and one wounded. The mortar men now rejoined and the platoon was settling down to a defensive position, wondering what had happened to the main body detailed to attack Mango Clump, when there was a crackle of rifle-fire right in their midst and a bullet whizzed between two of the Oxfords. One of Bisley's NCOs said to him: 'Look over there, sir.'

What they all saw, about twenty yards away, was the characteristic, long snout of a Japanese rifle projecting from the thick black line that betokened the mouth of a small Japanese bunker. Somehow this bunker had been missed. Like others of its kind it was a pit or deep trench, covered with a strong roof of logs, on top of which was piled as much earth as possible. The aperture was extremely narrow and the whole thing cunningly concealed.

Another shot told everyone that the enemy here was not the sort likely to be easily forced to surrender. The Jap at bay in his bunker fought like a tiger and did not yield. He had to be killed. 'Stone dead hath no fellow.' Casting about for a means, Holmes told some of the soldiers to see if there was any straw in the adjacent basha. They came back with two or three bundles and, with Holmes standing right on top of the bunker (and perfectly safe there), the straw was boldly stuffed into the aperture (not so safe!) and set alight, with the intention of smoking out the enemy.

As the last bundle was about to be pushed in, that ominous long snout shot out from the bunker once more and fired a couple of quick rounds. Bisley, who was in a dangerous position right in front of the bunker, fell, shot in the stomach. He was quickly dragged to a flank, but did not last long. His last words were: 'What a pity! What a pity!'

Holmes, angered by the gallant young man's death, now took command of the whole platoon. Climbing again on top of the bunker and lying flat, he was able, with a quick flick of the wrist, to slip two grenades through the aperture of the bunker. Another grenade was dropped by a corporal of the Oxfords who punched a hole in the roof. The grenades exploded and there was no more noise inside. The straw was still smouldering also and Holmes said to the corporal:

'That ought to put paid to them, but you never know with these rattlesnakes.'

At this moment Private Babb, the mortar man, volunteered to fire his mortar direct into the slit at close range. It was a brave thing to do and required, furthermore, skill and nerve. While everyone else stood well clear, Babb stationed himself fifteen yards from the bunker, laid the mortar against his side, with the barrel resting on a thick bamboo, and fired two bombs straight into the aperture. Each time he fired he was himself blown back by the force of the explosion. At first light some hours later four gruesomely mangled corpses were found in the bunker, so making a total bag for the night of fourteen dead – the entire garrison of Betel Hut. There was no victim left for Abdul.

Meanwhile, everyone was very worried about the situation at Mango Clump. Holmes, breaking wireless silence, spoke to Metcalfe and learnt to his surprise and disappointment that the attack had been called off, supposedly on higher authority. What Metcalfe proposed to do instead was to destroy Mango Clump by artillery fire at daybreak and he had asked Holmes to give visual indication of his own whereabouts for the benefit of the artillery observation officer. This Holmes did at first light by setting fire to the basha in their perimeter.

Meanwhile the Oxfords were digging like beavers and Holmes sited Bren-guns to cover each approach. He knew that the Japs would counter-attack as soon as possible, and in fact they made one of their stupid 'jitter' attacks just before day-break, uttering weird and supposedly terrifying noises and occasionally a deep 'Hallo' that echoed in ghostly fashion through the mangoes. At dawn Betel Hut was fired on from all directions, but Holmes still refused to disclose his dispositions. His wireless set, well dug in and served with cool efficiency by the two Oxford operators, providentially remained in action, though bullets kicked up dust all around.

Soon afterwards, as the light began to improve, Holmes saw a small, slow aircraft detach itself from the scenery to the north and fly very low towards them. He pointed it out to his men and said: 'Look, chaps, the gunner observation plane! Now for some sparks!'

Duly the sparks were kindled. A few single shells for ranging first, then the full weight of 'gun-fire' crashed down on Mango Clump with an accuracy that delighted the watching infantry-men. Eight guns – a battery – Holmes thought. Clods of earth, baulks of timber and pieces of metal were hurled into the morn-ing sunlight as the artillery 'Air Op', slowly and methodically flew up and down the gunners' line of fire, sending corrections to the guns by radio.

In twenty minutes or so nothing was apparently left of the defences of Mango Clump. Holmes's platoon relaxed and drank from their water-bottles. A few stray Japs continued to snipe at them from among the trees, but the Oxfords also had a sniper up.

At about 9 o'clock the sun had become unbearably hot and the flies were a trial, swarming alike over the living Englishmen and the dead Japs, who had begun to smell very offensively. Very soon after the hour, Betel Hut began to come under very unpleasant fire from heavy mortars in the wooded foothills to the east. Holmes began to take casualties, so he called up Metcalfe and asked if the gunners could locate and silence the mortars. This the gunners very efficiently did, but it was clear to Holmes that he would have to withdraw the men in the most exposed portion of his box. He sent them, at the double, to another copse about fifty yards to the rear.

Metcalfe, meantime, and perhaps his brigadier also, had decided to call it a day. The purpose of the raid had been fully achieved, though not by the means originally intended. He now gave orders to Holmes to pull out, under covering fire from the gunners. To disengage from an enemy at close quarters in full daylight is a perilous task, but the Oxfords, though tired, were cool and well trained. Holmes plotted a zigzag route for them, weaving from one copse to another, keeping low and moving at the double for short stretches. The Japs saw them, of course, and their mortars opened up again from the hills, but no one was hurt.

Extremely hot, extremely blown, they reached the chaung where White was waiting with their boats and there they all forthwith flopped into the water. There also they met Abdul again, his tortured, embittered face now wreathed in smiles. Running up to Holmes with arms upflung, he exclaimed:

'Allah be praised, sahib! You have avenged my cruel injustice. The blessing of Allah be upon the British soldiers!'

That same night Holmes sent in a party of picked scouts to observe the results in Mango Clump and Betel Hut. They reported having counted forty bodies and they brought back a rich haul of enemy equipment, some of which they were allowed to keep for their own use.

The successful little action was a tonic to Holmes's spirits. He felt purged of all ill humours and restored to his natural buoyancy. It was a good time to get out. The Arakan campaign was over and the sun had begun to set on the Japanese Empire. Two nights before, after a prolonged series of the most arduous assaults from their precarious footholds in the craggy hills of the Golden Fortress, 26th Division had at last stormed and won the daunting T-shaped bastion of Point 551, the final assaults having been made by 1st/8th Gurkhas and 2nd/7th Rajputs. Farther afield at Kohima and Imphal, Slim's other divisions, among whom were the 5th and 7th, had swung into a counter-offensive, which was to inflict upon the Japanese the most grisly and humiliating defeat in their history.

Having written a recommendation for the award of the Military Medal to Private Babb, Holmes broke the news of his departure to his comrades of V Force. Gus White said:

'In that case I shall go too. I'm fit again now and it's time I rejoined 44 Commando.'

Jemadar Shaffi took the news hardly, though he tried not to show his feelings and, in true Muslim fashion, said:

'It is the will of God, sahib; but I feel that you will be back again after the monsoon and we will go together victoriously to Akyab.'

Holmes found it hard to disabuse him and replied: 'You know that I must go wherever I am sent, Shaffi, but whatever happens I shall never forget you.'

The little Interpreter Shaffi and young Habibullah were more demonstrative. Habibullah was openly in tears and the interpreter on the brink of them. Danu Meah, the cook, made him the offering of a sumptuous breakfast and Mulvi Siddiq, his black eyes sombre above his sable beard, gave him a blessing from the Koran. Last of all, Holmes shook hands with Maurice Budd, to whom he handed over command of his little force, giving him a message for Luthera, who was in hospital with malaria. As the jeep drove off from Dewdrop Inn with Holmes, White and Khyber Khan the Gurkha guard presented arms and the little company of scouts stood waving in the dust.

At Maungdaw the three took a kisti out to the Dutch ship *General Michiels*, which was anchored in mid-stream and which in due course took them to Calcutta. After a spell of leave in Darjeeling, White went back to his commando and Holmes and Khyber Khan made a wearisome journey to a jungle-training battalion of his regiment in Central India. After a month or two there Holmes was deeply grieved to hear that both Jemadar Shaffi and Maurice Budd had been killed, the former by shell-fire while guiding a British patrol.

Soon afterwards, however, came the news that he really wanted. He was posted as second-in-command to his own original battalion, the 3rd/1st Punjabis, who (together with the author) were serving in 10th Indian Division in the Italian campaign. This was a battalion with a phenomenal war record, having had probably the longest period of active service of any Indian Army unit. After embarking for Egypt in September 1939, it had fought in the campaigns of the Western Desert, Abyssinia, Syria and Italy. Four of its commanding officers had been killed in action in a casualty list that ran to 1,651.

Back in Arakan Christison's divisions stepped out once more from their monsoon positions in mid-December. The Japanese, severely mangled in the great battle on the central front, had drawn heavily on their 28th Army for reinforcements, so that such resistance as they offered in Arakan was quickly overcome after a few sharp actions. Before the end of 1944 the whole of Mayu Peninsula was in British hands and then began that long series of seaborne landings, farther and farther south each time, in very difficult terrain and mazy river-mouths, known as the Battle of the Beaches. Here 3rd Commando Brigade, completed by the return of 1st and 42nd (Royal Marine) Commandos, came once more upon the scene, earning fresh laurels under the command of Brigadier Campbell Hardy, while 81st and 82nd West African Divisions, scrambling over terribly difficult and roadless ground, harried and pressed the enemy flank.

In 1945 came the great and decisive Battle of Mandalay, Slim's masterpiece, and soon afterwards many of the veterans of Arakan joined hands victoriously with those from the central front in Rangoon itself.

Appendix A

A Brief Note on the Indian Army
(Condensed from the author's *Springboard to Victory*)

Since the dust of time is beginning to obscure many landmarks once familiar to most of us, it will be helpful to the general reader to outline a few facts concerning the Indian Army, as far as they concern an understanding of the events in this book. The reader is reminded, in the first place, that at this time the Indian sub-continent, which was under British sovereignty, was not divided into the separate states of 'India' and 'Pakistan', as it unfortunately was after the grant of independence in 1947. Thus in this book the term 'Indian' means what it meant before 1947.

Indian Army formations and units were organized and trained in precisely the same way as those of the British Army. British officers and men formed a very large part of Indian divisions and the majority of the officers were British. Usually every infantry brigade was composed of one United Kingdom battalion and two Indian ones. Nearly all the field artillery was from Britain.

In the infantry units all the Indian rank and file, with a few exceptions, were recruited from two sources only: the Gurkhas (who were not Indians, but Nepalese) and a few martial races of Northern India – Punjabis, Rajputs, Dogras, Jats, Mahrattas, Garwhalis, Baluchis, Pathans and Sikhs. They came from village communities and were on the most cordial terms with the British soldier. The engineer units (Sappers and Miners), however, came from other parts of India also.

The Indian soldier was known as a sepoy, an old Anglo-Indian word adapted from the Urdu. The non-commissioned officers were havildars (equivalent to sergeants), naiks (equivalent to corporals) and lance-naiks. Above them was a grade peculiar to the Indian Army known as Viceroy's Commissioned

Officers (VCOs), who were junior in status to the King's Commissioned Officers. Except in the cavalry, their ranks were those of subedar (wearing two stars) and jemadar (one star). A very special VCO was the subedar-major, who was a man of great influence in the battalion and the CO's right-hand man in all matters concerning the sepoys. VCOs were usually men of long service, who had risen from the lower ranks. They commanded platoons and the equivalents of platoons in other arms.

Behind the fighting corps and divisions were a great many lines-of-communication troops, most of them untrained in arms.

Appendix B

Outline organization of an Army in the Field

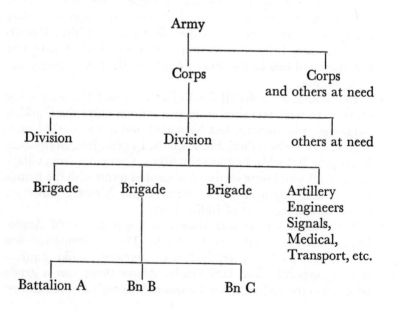

Sources

Diary, contemporary manuscript and personal narrative of Lt-Colonel D. C. B. Holmes, DSO.

Documentary:

Operation Instructions and Operation Orders of 3 Special Service Brigade.
Operation Orders of 44 (Royal Marine) Commando and 5 (Army) Commando.
Reports on Operations by 44 (RM) Commando.
War Diary of 5 Commando.
War Diary of 81 (West African) Division Reconnaissance Regiment.

Narratives, written and personal, from:

Major-General F. C. Horton, CB, OBE.
Brigadier A. E. Holt.
Brigadier G. H. Cree, CBE, DSO.
Mr A. R. White.
Mr J. R. G. Ross, MC.
Major O. N. St J. Hamlin, MBE.
Mr Ray Noble, MC.
Mr John Mitra.

Information on a number of matters kindly supplied by:

Major E. M. Sturges.
Mr D. C. P. Phelips, OBE.
Lt-Colonel T. L. F. Firbank, OBE.
Major A. S. Irwin, MC.
Major J. C. Stokes.
Mr H. W. Bond.
Mr R. J. Purdy, CMG, OBE.
Captain B. J. Grassby.
Mr D. W. Bastow.
Mr J. S. Greef.
Mr A. V. Macan.
Lt-Colonel B. Shattock, DSO.
H.M. Nautical Almanac Office.

Histories:

Those of 5th, 25th, and 26th Indian Divisions.
Regimental histories of The West Yorkshire and Lincolnshire Regiments.
History of the Royal West African Frontier Force.
Cabinet Office Official Histories, for operational background.
Report My Signals, by Antony Brett-James.
Burmese Outpost, by Anthony Irwin.

General Index

Military Index

Arranged alphabetically

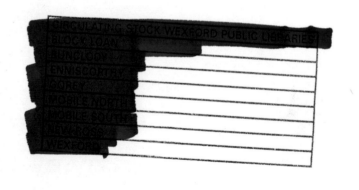